Picture the Past

Life in AMERICA'S FIRST CITIES

Sally Senzell Isaacs

Heinemann Library
Chicago, Illinois

© 2001 Reed Educational & Professional Publishing
Published by Heinemann Library,
an imprint of Reed Educational & Professional Publishing,
100 N. LaSalle, Suite 1010
Chicago, IL 60602
Customer Service 888-454-2279
Visit our website at www.heinemannlibrary.com

Produced for Heinemann Library by
    Bender Richardson White.
Editor: Lionel Bender
Designer: Ben White
Picture Researcher: Cathy Stastny
Media Conversion and Typesetting: MW Graphics
Production Controller: Kim Richardson

04 03 02 01
10 9 8 7 6 5 4 3 2 1

Printed in Hong Kong

Library of Congress Cataloging-in-Publication Data.
Issacs, Sally Senzell, 1950-
    Life in America's first cities/ Sally Senzell Isaacs.
        p. cm. – (Picture the past)
    Includes bibliographical references and index.
Summary: Introduces the daily lives of people who settled
in the first cities in the United States, discussing houses,
clothing, schools, and work.

ISBN 1-57572-315-8 (library binding)
1. United States-Social life and customs-1783-1865-Juvenile
literature. 2. City and town life-United States-History-19th
century-Juvenile literature. 3. Cities and towns-United
States-History-19th century-Juvenile literature.
(1. City and town life-History-19th century. 2. Cities and
towns-History-19th century. 3. United States-Social life and
customs-1783-1865.) I. Title.

E164 .I83 2000
973'0973'2-dc21

99-089882

Special thanks to Mike Carpenter, Scott Westerfield, and
Tristan Boyer Binns at Heinemann Library for editorial and
design guidance and direction.

Acknowledgments
The producers and publishers are grateful to the following
for permission to reproduce copyright material:
The Bridgeman Art Library: Library of Congress,
Washington D.C., 9; Museum of the City of New York,
pages 1, 3, 10, 17, 26, ; New York Historical Society, page 25.
Corbis: Corbis, pages 27, 30; Minnesota Historical Society,
page 24. Hulton Getty/Jacob A. Riis, page 19. Peter
Newark's American Pictures, pages 8, 13, 15, 18, 22, 23.
North Wind Pictures, pages 6, 11, 16, 28. Picture Research
Consultants/Smithsonian Institute, page 21.
Cover photograph: Peter Newark's American Pictures.

Every effort has been made to contact copyright holders
of any material reproduced in this book. Omissions will be
rectified in subsequent printings if notice is given to the
publisher.

Illustrations by John James, page 20; Gerald Wood, page
14; James Field, pages 12, 30; Nick Hewetson, page 7.
Map by Stefan Chabluk.
Cover make-up: Mike Pilley, Pelican Graphics.

Note to the Reader
Some words are shown in bold, **like this**.
You can find out what they mean by looking in the
glossary.

ABOUT THIS BOOK

This book tells about daily life in cities in the United States in the years 1800 to 1860. At this time, most Americans did not live in cities. They lived on farms. But cities were growing quickly. People looking for jobs moved to America's cities. They moved from farms. They moved from other countries, too.
We have illustrated the book with paintings and drawings from this time and with artists' ideas of how things looked then. In the 1850s, photography started to become popular, and we have included historic photographs from some of the first U.S. cities.

The Consultant
Special thanks go to Diane Smolinski for her help in the preparation of this series. Diane Smolinski has years of experience interpreting standards documents and putting them into practice.

The Author
Sally Senzell Isaacs is a professional writer and editor of nonfiction books for children. She graduated from Indiana University, earning a B.S. degree in Education with majors in American History and Sociology. For some years, she was the Editorial Director of Reader's Digest Educational Division. Sally Senzell Isaacs lives in New Jersey with her husband and two children.

CONTENTS

Towns Become Cities

Starting around 1800, many farmers moved to towns to escape the long hours, hard outdoor work, and loneliness of farming. They took jobs in factories, stores, and offices. Tens of thousands of people from Europe moved to new American towns to escape wars, lack of food, and poverty in their homelands. They hoped to earn money and give their children a better life. Slowly the towns grew into cities. By 1860, cities such as Boston and New York had more than 500 thousand people.

LOOK FOR THESE
The illustration of a city boy and girl sits alongside the title of each double-page story in the book.

The picture of an apartment building marks boxes with interesting facts about city life.

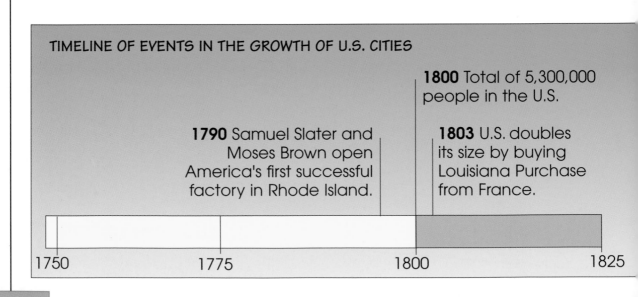

TIMELINE OF EVENTS IN THE GROWTH OF U.S. CITIES

1800 Total of 5,300,000 people in the U.S.

1790 Samuel Slater and Moses Brown open America's first successful factory in Rhode Island.

1803 U.S. doubles its size by buying Louisiana Purchase from France.

1750   1775   1800   1825

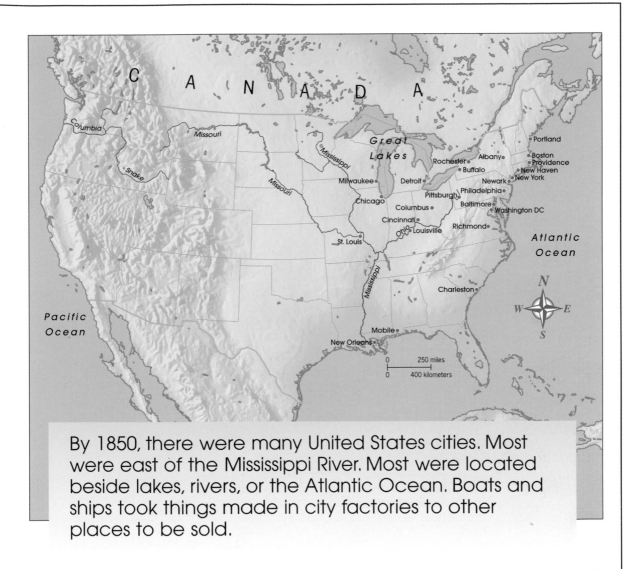

By 1850, there were many United States cities. Most were east of the Mississippi River. Most were located beside lakes, rivers, or the Atlantic Ocean. Boats and ships took things made in city factories to other places to be sold.

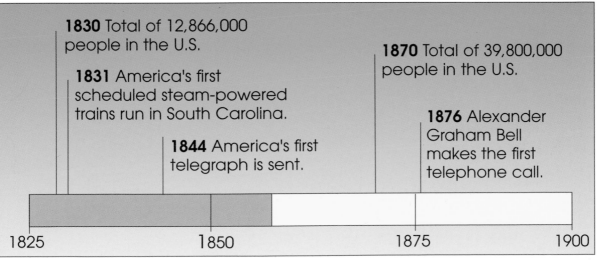

1830 Total of 12,866,000 people in the U.S.

1831 America's first scheduled steam-powered trains run in South Carolina.

1844 America's first telegraph is sent.

1870 Total of 39,800,000 people in the U.S.

1876 Alexander Graham Bell makes the first telephone call.

1825   1850   1875   1900

Busy Streets

A city was an exciting place. There were stores around every corner with things for sale. There were libraries, restaurants, theaters, and museums. Most of all, there were jobs.

Cities sometimes grew too fast. More and more people moved there. Stores could not get enough supplies for everyone. Builders could not build streets and houses fast enough. City streets became crowded with people, horses, and **carriages**. There were no traffic lights to help control the flow.

Large stores, like this one in Boston around 1850, sold everything needed for the home. Here, people shop for tablecloths, curtains, and material for clothes.

DIRTY STREET

Cities could be smelly places. People threw garbage out the front door. Then they let their pet pigs run free to eat the garbage.

This part of New York City had fancy stores and rich people. Poor people lived and shopped in another part of the city.

Getting News

There were no TVs, radios, movie theaters, or telephones. There were only newspapers. People heard most of their news from a neighbor—who heard it from a friend—who heard it from a traveler at the hotel.

City post offices displayed notices and kept copies of newspapers for everyone to read. News from towns far away often took several days to reach the city.

People mailed letters to one another. If a message had to reach someone quickly, a person went to the post office or **telegraph** office to send a **telegram**. The person told the message to a worker. The worker put the message in code and sent it through telegraph wires. A worker in another city read the code and wrote down the message.

Steam-driven printing presses, the electric telegraph, steamboats, and steam locomotives allowed news to travel fast and cities to grow.

Transportation

Cities were not very large. It took about thirty minutes to walk from one end of a city to the other. Still, Americans always liked to find faster ways to move. Some city people rode an **omnibus**. They sat on wooden benches and bounced along the bumpy streets.

Omnibuses and **carriages** move along Broadway, a busy street in New York City. An omnibus usually carried twelve people at a time.

Small boats carried goods and people to city harbors from towns upriver or along the coast.

Many people rode **stagecoaches** from one city to another. A trip could take three days, riding eighteen hours a day. It was sometimes easier to travel by boat. Boats were also better for sending loads of **factory**-made goods.

Homes and Houses

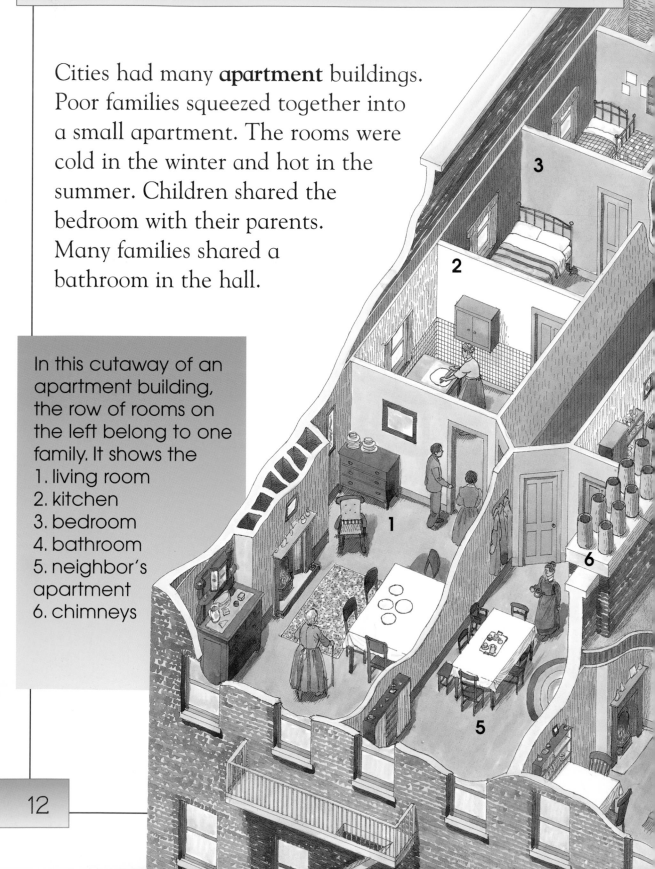

Cities had many **apartment** buildings. Poor families squeezed together into a small apartment. The rooms were cold in the winter and hot in the summer. Children shared the bedroom with their parents. Many families shared a bathroom in the hall.

In this cutaway of an apartment building, the row of rooms on the left belong to one family. It shows the
1. living room
2. kitchen
3. bedroom
4. bathroom
5. neighbor's apartment
6. chimneys

Some people lived in larger houses. There, children had their own bedrooms. The family ate together in the kitchen. For special times, they ate in a dining room. In 1850, not even the richest people had electric lights. They were not invented yet.

BATH TIME

To have a bath, people dragged a round tub into the kitchen or bathroom. They filled the tub with boiling water. They had a bath once a week.

Having one's own room for sleeping and playing was a luxury.
In 1850, houses did NOT have:
- air conditioning
- refrigerators
- televisions
- built-in bath tubs

Adults at Work

There were many kinds of jobs in the city. Some people worked in stores and offices. Some worked in schools and churches. Many men and women worked in **factories**. They stood by big machines twelve hours a day, six days a week.

This cutaway of a cotton **mill** shows:
1. men unloading raw cotton
2. and 3. women working spinning and weaving machines
4. men repairing machines

Factories made many things, such as clothes, shoes, guns, and clocks. They used machines powered by steam or running water. Each worker did one small job all day. In a skirt factory, one worker checked the thread. Another sewed the buttons. The jobs were boring and did not pay much.

FAST MACHINES

In earlier times, a shoemaker could make two to three pairs of shoes a day. A factory machine could make hundreds of shoes a day.

The first factories were noisy and dangerous. There was little fresh air.

15

Children at Work

Many city children had no time to go to school. They ran off to the **factory** each morning and worked there all day. They earned about two dollars a week. Their families needed this money to help pay for food and **rent**.

WORK DAY

5:00 A.M.: Wake up
6:00 A.M.: Start working
Noon : Quick break for lunch
6:00 P.M.: Go home to eat
8:00 P.M.: Go to sleep

Children did jobs needing tiny fingers. Often they had accidents with the machines.

Factory owners liked to **hire** children. They paid children less money than adults. Children could fit behind the machines to fix threads. They could sweep under the machines, too.

City children also worked in houses and on the streets. Some of them worked as **servants** for rich people.

Children sold newspapers and matches on the streets. They also delivered goods and cleaned chimneys.

School

Today, all children must go to school. Most schools are free. Before 1850, not every child went to school. Many children worked. Parents had to pay for school, except for very poor families. Free African-Americans living in the North were not allowed in the same schools with white children.

A school had only one room. Sometimes 100 students of all ages sat together.

The school day usually started with prayers and saluting the U.S. flag.

The classroom was usually very plain. In most schools, there were no maps or posters on the wall. Students sat on benches with writing tables in front of them. Children practiced writing words for many hours.

BOSTON SCHOOLS

Around 1850, Boston schools tried a new idea. Students of the same age sat together in the same classroom. Every student sat at a desk!

School Lessons

Boys and girls usually went to school together. Some schools were for girls only. Some were for boys only.

WRITING LESSONS

In most schools, children wrote on slates using slate pencils or sticks of white chalk.

To practice her school work at home, a young girl sewed these letters and numbers into a piece of cloth. She used a needle and lengths of colored threads.

WRITING PAPER

Some teachers made writing notebooks for the class. They folded paper and stitched it. Then they drew the writing lines.

In the classroom, some children wrote while others read out loud or practiced math problems. Children helped take care of the school. In winter, older children arrived early to start a fire and sweep the floor.

All children learned math, reading, writing, spelling, and history. They also learned good manners. In some schools, children had to stand in front of the teacher and spell their spelling words. Before speaking, children bowed to the teacher.

Clothes for Adults

Before the 1800s, men wore short pants, bunched at the knee. In the 1800s, long pants became the new style. Men still wore knee pants for sports, such as running and shooting.

Outdoors, most men and women usually wore hats.

Women would never think of wearing pants. They also thought it was wrong to show their ankles! They wore long dresses to go shopping and to go to fancy parties. They wore long dresses to work in **factories**. They even wore long dresses for swimming. Women wanted their waists to look tiny. They laced them up in **corsets**.

SHOES THAT FIT

Shoes were not made for right feet and left feet. There were no sizes for shoes either. A person tried on many, many shoes to find two that fit.

Women wore a **petticoat** and hoops made of steel wire and webbing under a dress to puff it out.

Clothes for Children

Some children had very fancy clothes. Boys wore vests and jackets trimmed with soft velvet. Girls wore **petticoats** under their dresses. They also wore long, lacy pants under their dresses. The pants were called drawers.

Children might wear these clothes to a birthday party or to go shopping in the city.

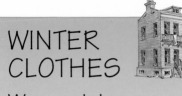

WINTER CLOTHES

Warm winter boots cost a lot of money. Poor parents stuffed straw and newspaper inside shoes to keep their children's feet warm.

Some families had no money to buy fancy clothes. A boy might wear the same pants and shirt year after year. A girl might wear the same dress. She always wore an apron over the dress to keep it as clean as possible.

In winter, rich parents bought their children thick coats and mittens or a muff to keep their hands warm.

Getting Food

People stored food for a short time in an ice box. This was a wooden chest with a block of ice inside. They bought ice on the street from a traveling salesman.

City homes had no room for gardens. People could not grow their own vegetables. They could not raise animals for meat. Trains and carts brought food from the farms to markets in the city.

ICE from ROCKLAND LAKE N.º 24.

BOTTLED FOODS

Some people put raw fish and vegetables in glass jars filled with **vinegar**. Others put cooked fruits and vegetables in glass jars. This kept these foods from **spoiling**.

There were no refrigerators in these days. People mostly used food that did not spoil, such as potatoes, onions, flour, and cornmeal. If they bought a turkey or fish, they cooked it right away. Raw eggs were too difficult to transport without being broken.

HOME DELIVERY

Many cities did not allow people to own cows. Farmers delivered milk and butter to city homes every day.

In this busy city neighborhood, people bought food every day from carts in the street.

27

A Simple Meal

At most houses, meals were very simple. There were few fresh fruits and vegetables. Many meals were just bread and potatoes.

Everyone in a family ate together. Meals were served and eaten in the living room. After the meal, plates, pots, and pans were washed by hand.

At Thanksgiving and other holidays, relatives might be invited for a meal. Everyone would help in the kitchen.

City Recipe—Potato Soup

Follow the instructions below to make potato soup as city people did in the early 1800s. Potato soup was an easy and cheap meal to make. This recipe makes enough hot potato soup for six helpings.

WARNING: Do not cook anything unless there is an adult to help you. Always ask an adult to do the cutting and cooking on a hot stove.

YOU WILL NEED
2 white potatoes, peeled and cut into small cubes
1 medium-size onion, cut in small pieces
2 tablespoons of butter
2 cups (480 ml) milk
2 teaspoons flour
1 teaspoon salt
dash of pepper

FOLLOW THE STEPS

1. Place the potatoes and onions in a pot and cover with water.
2. Cook until the potatoes are soft.
3. Pour the mixture in a strainer and drain off the water. Save the potatoes and onions.

4. Melt the butter in a pan.
5. Stir in the flour and cook gently for one minute.
6. Remove the pan from the heat and stir in the milk, salt, and pepper.

7. Put the pan back on the heat and stir until the milk boils.
8. Stir in the potato and onion mixture. Heat for two more minutes.
9. Serve hot in bowls, with bread.

How Cities Changed

From around 1850, America's cities grew bigger very quickly. More people moved to cities from farms and from other countries. By 1860, cities were **hiring** garbage collectors, police, and fire fighters to make the streets safer and healthier. **Factories** became safer, too. Young children were no longer allowed to work in factories and **mills**. Instead, they all went to school.

BIGGEST U.S. CITY

In 1800, there were 60,000 people living in New York City. By 1900, there were two million people living in the city.

This photo shows a street scene in New York City, 1865.

Glossary

apartment one of many rooms or sets of rooms within a building in which people live. In cities, run-down apartment buildings are known as tenements.

carriage type of transportation pulled by horses that was used to carry people and goods

corset clothing worn by women under a dress to squeeze the waist and make it look smaller

factory building where things are made in large numbers or amounts, usually with the help of machines

hire to take on and pay someone to do a job

mill factory where products, such as cloth, paper, glass, furniture, and steel, are made

omnibus wooden car pulled by horses that had several seats for passengers to travel round towns and cities

petticoat thin, lightweight skirt worn under a skirt or dress

rent money paid to live or work in someone else's building or house

servant someone who works in another person's house, usually cooking, cleaning, and serving

spoil to become rotten

stagecoach boxlike car pulled by horses in which people traveled long distances

telegram message sent by telegraph

telegraph machine that sends messages over wires in the form of a code

vinegar sour liquid usually made from wines

More Books to Read

An older reader can help you with these books:
Thompson, Ware. *Cities: The Building of America*. Danbury, Conn.: Children's Press, 1997.
Toynton, Evelyn. *Growing up in America: 1830-1860*. Brookfield, Conn.: Millbrook Press, Incorporated, 1995.

Index

JAPANESE COUNTRY TEXTILES

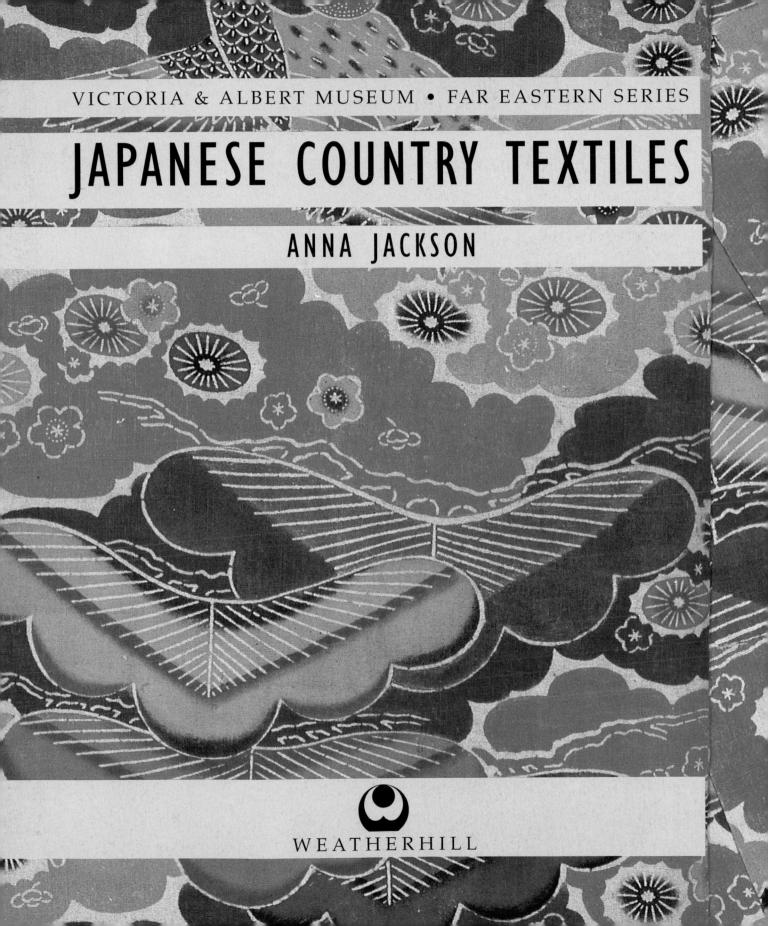

VICTORIA & ALBERT MUSEUM • FAR EASTERN SERIES

JAPANESE COUNTRY TEXTILES

ANNA JACKSON

WEATHERHILL

To the memory of Lisa Bailey,
a cherished friend and colleague

First published by V&A Publications, 1997
First Weatherhill edition, 1997

Published by Weatherhill, Inc., of New York and Tokyo,
with editorial offices at 568 Broadway, Suite 705, New York,
N.Y. 10012, by special arrangement with the Victoria and
Albert Museum

ISBN 0-8348-0396-8

Illustrations

FRONT COVER Early 20th-century fisherman's celebratory
robe (*maiwai*). Cotton with stencilled decoration (*katazome*).

BACK COVER Detail from a late 19th-century length of
fabric. Bast fibre (*asa*) woven with selectively resist-dyed
yarns (*kasuri*).

PAGE 1 Detail from a late 19th-century cotton cloth,
either a bedding cover (*futonji*) or a covering cloth (*yutan*).
Freehand paste-resist decoration (*tsutsugaki*).

PAGE 3 Detail from a 19th-century robe.
Cotton with stencilled decoration (*bingata*).

Designed by Harry Green

Printed by C S Graphics, Singapore

Contents

Preface

Detail from a 19th-century stencil (see fig. 60).

The Victoria and Albert Museum is fortunate to have a large and diverse collection of Japanese textiles. In addition to silk *kimono*, Buddhist robes, gift cloths and a large variety of other items, the Museum has a wonderful group of what are generally categorized as 'country' or 'folk' textiles. This collection is one of the best in the world, but has not been published in detail before.[1] The main objective of this book is to bring these objects to the attention of a wider audience.

The book is divided into four chapters. The first examines the way in which the separate category of 'country textiles' has been constructed in the twentieth century, discussing in particular the work of Yanagi Sōetsu and the Folk Craft movement. This problematic classification, it is argued, has limited our understanding of the original function and meaning of these objects. The chapter also explores the circumstances by which the collection at the V&A was acquired. The second chapter considers the social, religious, political and economic significance of the textiles within the communities that produced and consumed them. The specific techniques used to make and pattern the textiles are the subject of chapter three. The book concludes with a brief examination of textile production since the Meiji period, and the work of a number of contemporary makers who look to traditional textile practices in the creation of their work.

The publication of this book owes much to my colleagues in the Far Eastern Department, who have encouraged me and shared their knowledge with me. I would particularly like to thank Rupert Faulkner and Verity Wilson for their thoughtful reading of the text, Andrew Bolton for organizing the photographic programme, and Ian Thomas for taking the marvellous pictures. I am also very grateful to Mary Butler and Miranda Harrison of V&A Publications for all their help in making this book a reality.

NOTES

1. The only article that has been published on the collection is Verity Wilson, 'Country Textiles from Japan and the Ryūkyūan Islands in the Victoria and Albert Museum', *Orientations*, vol. 14, no. 7, 1983, pp 28–42.

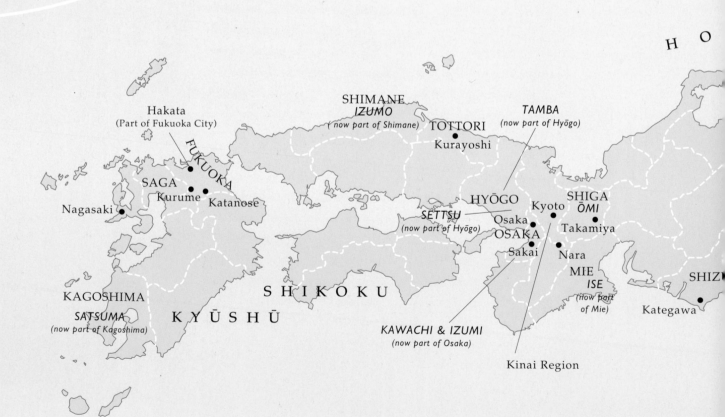

CHINA

SEA OF
JAPAN

KOREA

JAPAN

PACIFIC OCEAN

TAIWAN

N

N

H O

Hakata
(Part of Fukuoka City)

SHIMANE
IZUMO
(now part of Shimane)

TOTTORI
Kurayoshi

TAMBA
(now part of Hyōgo)

FUKUOKA

SAGA
Kurume   Katanose

Nagasaki

HYŌGO

SETTSU
(now part of Hyōgo)

Osaka

OSAKA

Sakai

Kyoto

SHIGA
ŌMI

Takamiya

Nara

MIE
ISE
*(now part
of Mie)*

Kategawa

SHIZ

KAGOSHIMA

SATSUMA
(now part of Kagoshima)

KYŪSHŪ

S H I K O K U

KAWACHI & IZUMI
(now part of Osaka)

Kinai Region

HOKKAIDŌ

Hakodate

Tsugaru
Peninsula

AOMORI

H Ū

Shōnai
Plain

YAMAGATA

NIIGATA
ECHIGO

Yonezawa

Ojiya

IBARAKI

Tokyo
Edo

Yūki

Bōsō Peninsula

KEY

AOMORI   Prefecture

ECHIGO   Province (former name)

Amami
Oshima

KAGOSHIMA

R Y Ū K Y Ū   I S L A N D S

Kijoka

Okinawa Island

Shuri

Yaeyama
Islands

Miyako Islands

OKINAWA

N

NOTES ON CAPTIONS

For continuity the term 'robe' has been used to describe all full-length garments from the Ryūkyū Islands, even when their construction is the same as mainland *kimono*.

The provenance of the textiles is stated when known. In some instances the old provincial name is given, but the modern day prefectural name always follows in brackets.

All measurements are in centimetres (length × width). In the case of garments the length is the distance from the base of the neck to the hem, and the width the distance across the shoulders from sleeve end to sleeve end.

NOTES ON JAPANESE NAMES AND PRONUNCIATION

Japanese names are given in the Japanese order: family name followed by given name. Japanese terms are italicized throughout.

Consonants in Japanese are pronounced in much the same way as they are in English, the vowels as they are in Italian. There is a difference, however, between the long and short u/ū and o/ō, the macron over the vowel indicating the longer form. The shorter form 'u' is pronounced as in 'cruet', the longer form 'ū' as in 'boot'; the shorter form 'o' as in 'hot', the longer form 'ō' as in 'oar'. Macrons have been used throughout the text except on the frequently found place names such as Tokyo, Kyoto, Osaka (strictly speaking Tōkyō, Kyōto and Ōsaka).

Chronology

Nara Period	710–794
Heian Period	794–1185
Kamakura Period	1185–1336
Muromachi Period	1336–1573
Momoyama Period	1573–1615
Edo Period	1615–1868
Meiji Period	1868–1912
Taishō Period	1912–1926
Shōwa Period	1926–1989
Heisei Period	1989–

1 | Definition and Acquisition

1 Farmer's coat. Cotton quilted in cotton thread (*sashiko*). Late 19th century. 124.5 × 122.0. FE.30–1982.

Japan has an extremely rich textile history. The arts of weaving, dyeing and embroidery have always played a crucial role in determining the cultural climate of the country, and continuing respect for these traditional skills has secured Japan's present position as a major force in the world of textile design. The sumptuous *kimono* that were such a feature of the Japanese urban environment in the Edo (1615–1868) and Meiji (1868–1912) periods have been an important subject of aesthetic appreciation and scholarly investigation. These sophisticated silk garments were not the only form of Japanese dress, however, nor the only focus for the application of textile skills. The less affluent, particularly those living in rural areas, wore and used other kinds of textiles. The need for mobility, warmth and protection was central to the creation of garments such as the farmer's coat in fig. 1. Although similar in basic cut, it is very different in style and purpose to a fashionable city *kimono*. The sleeves are tapered to allow for ease of movement, and the quilting provides extra durability. Textiles such as this are worthy of attention not only for their particular beauty and for their use of often complex techniques, but also for the contribution they make to our understanding of Japanese social and cultural history.

The objects that are the focus of this study are often known as 'country' textiles. The majority of them were made in the nineteenth and twentieth centuries and, as the name suggests, most were made away from the metropolitan weaving areas. They tend to be of cotton or linen-like fibres rather than of silk, and are characteristically coloured with indigo-blue dye. Patterning is usually achieved through resist-dyeing techniques rather than embroidery. These textiles are also seen to belong to the broader category of folk art, generally defined as art made by the lower classes for use by the lower classes. The Victoria and Albert Museum has a large and varied collection of over 130 country textiles. These include lengths of fabric (see fig. 4) as well as smaller fragments and samples (see fig. 8), some of which have been mounted in albums, as in fig. 9. The collection also includes domestic items, particularly bed covers (see fig. 15) and garments. The exuberantly decorated robe in fig. 2, which would have been worn by a fisherman, seems very different in style, patterning and purpose to the kind of *kimono* worn by rich city dwellers. Yet when one looks more closely at how the term 'country textiles' has been defined, and at the objects that have been classified within its parameters, certain problems emerge. Although the length of fabric in fig. 3 has many of the hallmarks of a country textile, with its linen-like fibre, indigo-blue ground and resist-dyed patterning, it would not have been part of a garment worn by a country peasant. It is a fragment of a summer *kimono* that would have belonged to a wealthy member of the urban classes. The piece of cotton fabric shown

2 Fisherman's celebratory robe (*maiwai*). Cotton with stencilled decoration (*katazome*). Early 20th century. 136.0 × 131.0. FE.102–1982.

3 Length of fabric. Bast fibre (*asa*) with freehand paste-resist decoration (*tsutsugaki*). 19th century. 74.2 × 31.0.
138–1968.

4 Length of fabric. Cotton with freehand paste-resist decoration (*tsutsugaki*). Late 19th century. 54.0 × 31.8.
T.202–1964.

5 Ainu robe (*attush*). Elm-bark fibre (*ohyō*) with cotton cloth appliqué and cotton thread embroidery. Hokkaidō, mid-19th century. 128.5 × 128.0. T.99–1963.

in fig. 4, also with an indigo-blue ground and patterned in a similar way, is a good example of what is usually referred to as a country textile. Its rural origins appear to be born out by the legend written on the sheet of paper in which the fabric is wrapped, which reads 'Place of manufacture: the regions'.[1] However, while the pattern of drums, pines and waterfall on the latter piece has been applied more freely than the elegant chrysanthemums on the former, the distinction between them is by no means clear.

What *is* clear is that the labelling of Japanese textiles as 'country' or 'folk' embraces a wide range of objects, made under differing social and economic conditions for a variety of purposes. The robe in fig. 5, for example, was made by an Ainu woman in Hokkaidō, the northernmost island of Japan. The Ainu are an aboriginal people who live primarily by hunting and gathering. Their belief in the presence of animal spirits effects all aspects of their lives, and is woven into the textiles they wear. Robes such as this, known as *attush*, are made from fibres taken from the inner bark of the elm tree. The motifs that decorate them serve a symbolic function, protecting the wearer against evil spirits.

Also classified as a country textile is the stencilled cloth from Okinawa, called *bingata*. Far removed socially, politically, religiously and geographically from the Ainu culture of Hokkaidō, Okinawa is the largest of over seventy islands that form the Ryūkyū archipelago to the south of mainland Japan. The robe shown in fig. 6 would have been worn by a member of Ryūkyūan royalty, and would have been made to order in the palace workshops.

What is it that links these two contrasting cultures and the very distinct roles played by the textiles they produce? How is it that garments worn by royalty are classified as folk art? The connections do not lie in the meaning these cultural artefacts had when they were first produced, but in the way they have been defined during the twentieth century. The most important influence on the interpretation of such objects has been Yanagi Sōetsu (1889–1961), the founder of the Japanese Folk Craft movement. But he was not the first person to study and collect examples of everyday material culture from pre-industrial Japan. The American zoologist Edward Morse (1838–1925), who made his first visit to Japan in 1877, amassed an enormous collection of objects which he took back to his native Boston.[2] In 1913 the ethnologist Yanagida Kunio (1875–1962) began to encourage the study of Japanese traditional culture. Yanagida spent much of his life researching, lecturing and writing, eventually publishing a thirteen volume work entitled *Bunrui Minzoki Goi (Classified Glossary of Folklore)*.

Like Yanagida, Yanagi Sōetsu was intent on preserving crafts which he believed were under threat from increased industrialization. Dramatic economic, political and social changes took place in Japan at the end of the nineteenth century, as the country sought to establish parity with western powers. It was not until after the victories of the Sino-Japanese and the Russo-Japanese wars of 1894–5 and 1904–5, however, that rapid industrialization and urbanization took place. In the early decades of the twentieth century, the apparent conflict between western and indigenous ideas caused a growing unease that slowly developed into the socio-political nationalism that led to the country's imperialist ambitions. Although Yanagi himself did not indulge in, or support, the military rhetoric, it is important to realise that his ideas took shape within a broader

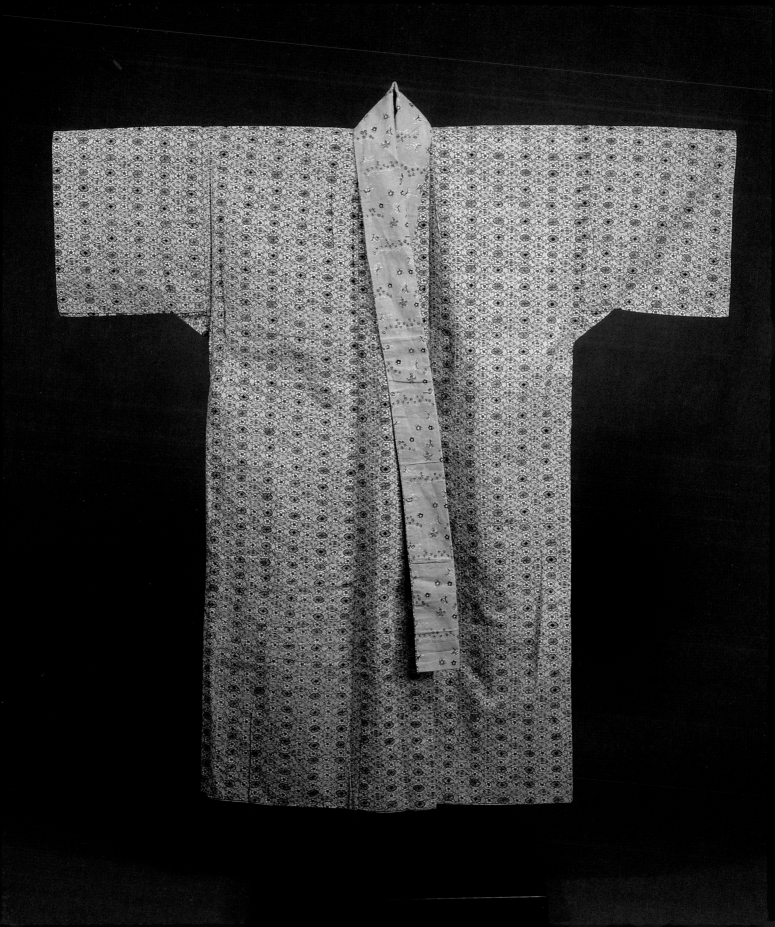

intellectual context in which questions of Japanese originality and national identity were being debated and defined.

While the approach of Yanagida, and Morse before him, was basically scientific, Yanagi's study and promotion of Japanese crafts was aesthetic. His philosophy, and the Folk Craft movement he founded, have much in common with the British Arts and Crafts movement and the ideas of William Morris (1834–96). Although Yanagi, a great self-publicist, sought to stress the originality of his ideas, Morris was undoubtedly a strong influence.[3] Both movements looked to a golden age of the past in the face of a disturbing present in which, it was believed, morality was being destroyed by the forces of capitalism. Yanagi and Morris shared a Utopian vision of rural communities in which craftsmen worked in harmony with nature. For both of them nature signified beauty, and within beauty was to be found 'truth'.

Yanagi learnt much about William Morris from his English friend, the potter Bernard Leach (1887–1979), whom he first met in 1910. Leach also introduced Yanagi to the work of John Ruskin and William Blake, whose mysticism the latter came to admire deeply. The Englishman also encouraged Yanagi's growing interest in Asian art. Discussions with Leach and with the potters Hamada Shōji (1894–1978) and Kawai Kanjirō (1890–1966) led Yanagi, in 1925, to coin the word '*mingei*' to describe the work of the craftsmen he and his friends admired. This was an abbreviated term derived from *minshū* (common people) and *kōgei* (craft). Yanagi deliberately translated *mingei* into English as 'folk craft' rather than folk art, writing:

> Mingei is a new word…Etymologically, it has the sense of 'the art of the common classes'. In fact I conceive of it in opposition to the arts of the aristocracy…*Mingei* has two characteristics: the first is functionalism, the second is ordinariness…objects that are luxurious, expensive and made in very small numbers do not belong in this category. The makers of mingei are not famous people but anonymous craftsmen.[4]

In 1927 Yanagi published his *Way of Crafts*. In this and many of his other publications he set out his aesthetic theories. His work became known in the West through its promotion by Leach, who published a collection of his friend's writings in 1972 under the title *The Unknown Craftsman: A Japanese Insight into Beauty*. In 1936 the Japanese Folk Craft Museum was opened in Tokyo as a place where, Yanagi stated, people would 'come into contact with the religion of beauty'. The objects on display would also, he believed, provide inspiration for craftsmen of the future because they showed what was 'true work'.

For an object to be labelled 'folk', it needed to meet a number of criteria established by Yanagi. To qualify, objects had, above all, to be functional: 'Beauty [in crafts] is that identified with use. It is beauty born of use. Apart from use there is no beauty of craft. Therefore, things made that do not stand up to use or that ignore utility can barely be expected to contain this kind of beauty'. Folk crafts also needed to be made anonymously, by hand, using natural materials, traditional methods and designs, and simple forms. An object had to be one of many similar pieces and to be inexpensive. Of a farmer's coat (see fig. 1) Yanagi said: 'This needlework looks like added decoration but it is nothing of the sort. Its charm is in its appropriateness to use and the strength of its stitching. The delightful patterning is incidental and utterly suitable. There is no concept of decor for its own sake'.

6 Lined robe. Cotton with stencilled decoration (*bingata*). Shuri, Okinawa, Ryūkyū Islands, 19th century. 121.0 × 120.0. T.296–1960.

Yanagi's particular admiration for *bingata* stemmed from what he called its 'funda-mental honesty' (see fig. 6). By this he seems to be referring to the fact that the pattern-ing of *bingata* relied exclusively on stencil dyeing and was not augmented by other dyeing methods or by embroidery – it did not, therefore, have the combination of tech-niques often seen on fashionable Edo-period city *kimono*. In his appreciation of *bingata* Yanagi, rather curiously, appears not to have understood the conditions under which the fabric was made, believing that *bingata* dyeing was carried out by women when in fact it was done exclusively by men. He also erroneously believed that 'these textiles were available to all and were not for the upper classes'.[5]

A basic misunderstanding of production and usage informed the acceptance of *bin-gata* as *mingei*. When we look more widely at the textiles and other artefacts that have been gathered together under the folk-craft umbrella, a serious disparity emerges between the concept and the actual objects. To begin with, all textiles are functional. The most stunning of silk *kimono* were made to be worn. The makers of country textiles are indeed unknown, but so are most of those who made artefacts for rich merchants and the military aristocracy. In pre-industrial Japan everything was made by hand with natural materials. It may seem that textiles fall more naturally into the category of folk craft because, unlike ceramics or lacquerwork, they tend to be made in the home. Cer-tainly cloth was spun and woven, predominantly by women, within rural households. Dyeing of textiles was done outside the home, however, by professional male artisans who spent many years developing their considerable skill and expertise. Furthermore, the patterning methods are often extremely complex and time-consuming. While the designs do suggest the use of particular textiles, the exuberance of colour and pattern on those made for celebration reflect a love of decoration rather than any overriding considerations of function (see fig. 2).

Many of the forms and techniques of country textiles can be seen as traditional. They would have been handed down through each generation of a family or passed on from artisan to apprentice. The motifs that decorate many of the textiles are auspicious ones intended to bring good luck. The meanings of such motifs and the beliefs that underlie them would also have been passed on from one generation to the next. The word 'tra-dition', however, suggests something that is unaffected by change, something that is static and that lives outside historical processes. This is not true of these, or indeed any, objects. By emphasizing the traditional quality of the objects he admired, Yanagi effec-tively denied them a place within their own, extremely dynamic, time. He isolated them for their artistic significance, forgetting that objects such as the textiles examined in this book could simultaneously perform a variety of social, religious, political and economic roles within the communities that produced and consumed them.

Yanagi believed that commerce destroyed good craftsmanship. He blamed what he saw as a decline in the quality of Ryūkyūan textiles in the Meiji period, for example, on 'the spread of wholesale trading' and the emphasis on the 'profit-making motive'.[6] Yet the Edo period witnessed the growth of an extensive network of trading routes and the distribution of large volumes of goods. Many farming communities turned to textile production because it provided a good source of income, and ensured far greater prof-its than could be made by cultivation of the land. The consumers of these textiles were also a diverse group. Certainly many fabrics were woven and dyed to be used by immediate community members. But rich merchants and even *samurai* also wore and used them. Indeed, such customers were dependant on the work of anonymous craftswomen, for it was only the *daimyō* (the military ruler of each province) who had their own artisans to make goods for them. Sometimes members of rural communities could not afford to use the cloth they wove (see fig. 36) and it was sold, through wholesalers, to rich urban dwellers. Such textiles were neither inexpensive nor ordinary.

Ultimately, Yanagi did not follow his own theories by collecting every kind of functional object in a belief that it was innately beautiful. What he collected and classified as *mingei* was essentially what he liked. It is important to consider his status in relation to his collecting. Unlike the anonymous rural craftsman that he championed, Yanagi was born into the Japanese elite. His decision to collect objects from the fringes of society, whether from regional cultures or from peoples who were subjugated to the Japanese (such as the Koreans, the Ryūkyūans and the Ainu), was not a rejection but a reflection of his own social and cultural background. He did not collect from within these cultures, but from a position of superiority and authority above and outside of them. He occupied the intellectual and ethical highground from which he could be all-knowing about the 'other'. As such, his activities echo those of western imperialists who collected 'primitive' art from 'uncivilized' or 'yet to be civilized' societies.

In fact, Yanagi's system of classification was only meaningful in the context of his own time. When the objects that Yanagi so admired were actually made, the dichotomy of rural and urban, high art and low art, did not exist. There was a difference between things made for rural peasants and those made for the urban rich, and so artistic hierarchies of a sort did operate. However, there was not a strict polarization between different types of artistic production. A variety of textiles were created in a variety of ways, for a variety of consumers. The categories of 'art' and 'craft' were adopted from the West, and were still fairly new at the time that Yanagi was forming his philosophy. Yanagi believed that he had discovered in folk crafts something that could provide salvation from what he saw as the spiritual decay of modern society. Folk craft was, however, a concept that Yanagi had effectively invented, for it was only within, and in opposition to, a highly urbanized and industrialized society that the notion of folk craft had any meaning.[7]

Although it is difficult to discern any common characteristics belonging to the objects that Yanagi defined as *mingei*, they do seem to share a certain directness. They do not have the ostentation of much of the art created for the castles of the military elite. Nor do they share the pre-occupation with ever-changing fashion that is the hallmark of the 'floating world' of the city.[8] The aesthetic found in so-called folk objects is also far removed from that which informed the sophisticated pieces of technical virtuosity produced in the Meiji period.[9]

Similarities have been drawn between Yanagi's language and aims and those of Walter Gropius (1883–1969), who in 1919 founded the Bauhaus, one of the most influential design schools of the twentieth century.[10] In considering the apparent qualities of particular objects, we need to recognize how twentieth-century critics have shaped our aesthetic values. The directness we perceive in 'folk craft' objects appeals to us looking, as we inevitably do, through our late twentieth-century eyes. The objects have a simplicity, which received artistic opinion throughout most of this century has maintained is a

7 Model robe. Cotton with cotton cloth appliqué and cotton thread embroidery. Hakodate, Hokkaidō, early 20th century. 46.0 × 57.7. T.264–1910.

hallmark of good design. Simplicity is no longer a relative concept, but an ideological one. Influential critics and designers such as Adolf Loos, Herbert Read, Le Corbusier and Gropius have decreed that ornamentation is equivalent to degeneration, and that simplicity is the goal of civilization.[11]

Although perceptions and interpretations of the past or present cannot be overlooked, we need to be aware of how our understanding of material culture is formed. Meaning is never fixed; it is constantly shifting. The problem of definition briefly outlined above does not make the study of these textiles any less valid, but the desire to categorize them so rigidly should to be tempered. It is necessary to step outside the romantic world of Yanagi and its failure to address the social structure and economic conditions within which these textiles were originally made and consumed.

Many of the objects that were collected by Yanagi are now in his Japanese Folk Craft Museum. The textiles that are the focus for this study are also from a particular museum collection: however, the objects in the V&A were acquired at different times by different curators, whose criteria for acquisition were often quite haphazard and informed by a variety of ideas. In contrast to the Japanese Folk Craft Museum, therefore, the formation of the collection has not been guided by one overarching aesthetic principle. The V&A acquired its first Japanese textiles in 1865. They were given to the Museum by Queen Victoria, who had received them five years earlier as part of a large diplomatic gift from the last but one *shōgun*, Tokugawa Iemochi (r.1858–1866).[12] All these early acquisitions were of silk textiles, the majority embroidered or brocaded. It was not until 1910 that the first objects of concern to this study were acquired: a collection of Ainu garments, an example of which is shown in fig. 7. Although it was felt that the 'interest [of these Ainu garments] is largely ethnographic', they were acquired because 'the embroidered patterns have...some further interest for their primitive character'.[13] It is likely that the Museum's decision to acquire the textiles was influenced by the display of an Ainu village at the Japan-British Exhibition that took place in London that year. A memorandum written when the objects were acquired suggested that relevant information could be found in the work of the Reverend John Batchelor (1854–1944). Batchelor worked as a missionary among the Ainu, and published two books about them in 1892 and 1901. The fascination for these 'hairy aborigines' engendered by Batchelor's books may well have helped persuade the Museum to accept this gift of Ainu textiles.[14]

The Museum's attitude to Ainu culture seems to have changed little between 1910 and 1965, when the *attush* robe seen earlier (fig. 5) was acquired. A note in the acquisition records reads, 'although Ainu textiles are too ethnographic to be of more than marginal interest to us, one fine garment is well worth having'.[15] Another important factor in this acquisition was undoubtedly the identity of the donor. The robe was given to the Museum by Bernard Leach who, at the time, was vigorously promulgating the ideas of Yanagi in the West. Indeed, the majority of the country textiles in the V&A were acquired in the 1950s and 1960s, when Yanagi's theories were being disseminated outside Japan. These objects were sold or given to the V&A by the Dutch anthropologist Jaap Langewis.[16] Langewis first wrote to the Museum from Kyoto in December 1956, stating that he was 'carrying out research work on antique methods of Japanese hand-dyeing and hand-weaving' and that he wondered if the Museum would be interested in acquiring any items. With his letter he enclosed a sample of resist-dyed cloth (fig. 8).[17] George Wingfield Digby (1911–1989), the Keeper of the Textiles Department, replied to Langewis on 7 January 1957, saying that he would certainly be interested in acquiring a small but good collection, and commenting that he had always regarded such textiles 'as extremely beautiful'.[18] This was the start of a remarkable friendship between the two men, which was to leave the Museum with an exceptional collection of Japanese indigo-dyed and *bingata* textiles.[19]

In a memorandum dated 15 June 1964 to the Director of the V&A, requesting money to be made available for a further purchase, Wingfield Digby writes:

> The collection [of three bed covers, four samples and thirteen scrolls] is an extremely fine one of textiles in the Mingei tradition on which Mr Langewis has made himself an expert during his long stay in Japan. I feel that this collection would be of unique

8 Fragment. Bast fibre (*asa*) woven with selectively resist-dyed yarns (*kasuri*), the warp yarns hand-tied, the weft yarns board-clamped (*itajime*). Ōmi Province (Shiga Prefecture), mid – late 19th century. 17.6 × 16.4. T.118–1957.

value for us to acquire, particularly in view of the new Department of Oriental Art which is now in the foreseeable future. Such a collection probably could not be made again; certainly not outside Japan, and the Mingei movement in Japan is well financed by buyers at high prices. Whilst there are very few museums in Europe and America who would want to buy this collection, I feel certain that Mr Langewis would be able to sell it, and I think it is true that owing to our previous friendly relations with him we are getting first offer of it.[20]

This memo is significant. Firstly it reveals the pioneering nature of the collection being built up at the V&A. It also shows that Wingfield Digby was well aware of the *mingei* movement and the theories informing Langewis's collecting criteria. Indeed, Wingfield Digby was a friend of Bernard Leach, as well as an important collector of his work and that of other leading British and Japanese potters.[21]

One interesting insight into the East-West cultural dialogue is contained in a letter from Wingfield Digby to Langewis, in which he mentions that 'his wife saw a dress brought back from Japan by Mrs Bernard Leach, which is made from two kimono lengths of Kurume kasuri'. He continues:

> this is quite inexpensive in Japan and if you could obtain and send one and a half or two kimono lengths of Kurume kasuri with identical patterns, dark and light blue, with the smaller pattern as made for older people in Japan, we should be extremely pleased. It makes up into a very pretty dress in Western style.[22]

Japanese folk textiles had found, it seems, a new context as a fabric worn by women in British intellectual and artistic circles.

The memo of 1964 also reveals that, in Japan at least, *mingei* was firmly established within accepted artistic canons. These humble crafts were, by this time, fetching very high prices. Yanagi may have condemned the economics of the market place, but folk craft objects had become highly sought-after commodities. The interest in *mingei* textiles is manifest in the creation of books such as that shown in fig. 9, published in 1974

9 Book of textile samples. Late 19th – early 20th century, book compiled in 1974. 22.0 × 16.0. FE.40–1985.

黄八丈（明治初年頃）

（柳宗悦氏母堂の使用されしもの）

Hachijojima:
silk.

10 Book of textile samples. Late 19th – early 20th century, book compiled in 1932. 31.4 × 21.4. T.172–1963.

as a limited edition of 200. It contains 300 assorted striped and checked cotton textiles dating from the late nineteenth to the early twentieth century, each provenanced and approximately dated.

Originally sample books were created from off-cuts when fabric was first produced. Within the urban community such books served to illustrate to potential customers the various styles and techniques of particular workshops. The same was also true in rural communities, where the books also served as a personal record for the maker and as a way of passing on skills to the next generation. In this century, not only have such sample books been themselves collected, but collectors have created their own. The example shown in fig. 10 was compiled in 1932 by Rokurō Uemura, who subsequently gave it to Bernard Leach. The samples include not only woven cotton and Ainu elm-bark fibre, but also examples of striped and checked silk. The sample on the page illustrated here is invested with an even greater significance, for it is apparently from a garment worn by Yanagi's mother. These books are as much evidence of the nature of collecting as they are of the skills of textile creation.

The new curatorial section of the V&A to which Wingfield Digby refers in his memo was not to become a reality until 1970, when the Far Eastern Department was created from the Japanese, Chinese and Korean holdings of the Museum's materials-based collections. Since that time the department has sought to build on the legacy of Wingfield Digby and Langewis, particularly in the area of Japanese costume.[23] The main aim of this book is to illustrate some of the wonderful textiles from the V&A's collection and to reveal something of their original production, their continuing significance and their lasting beauty.

NOTES

1. This was probably written by a dealer eager to exploit the growing marketability of these kinds of textiles in the mid-twentieth century.

2. Much of Morse's collection is housed in the Peabody Museum in Salem, Massachusetts. The ceramics from his collection are now in the Boston Museum of Fine Arts.

3. See Brian Morean, *Lost Innocence: Folk Craft Potters of Onta, Japan* (Berkeley, Los Angeles and London: University of California Press 1984), pp 9–11, and Yūko Kikuchi, 'The Myth of Yanagi's Originality: The Formation of Mingei Theory in its Social and Historical Context', *Journal of Design History*, vol.7, no.4, 1994, pp 247–66.

4. Yanagi Sōetsu, *Mingei Yonjūnen* (Tokyo: Iwanami Shoten 1984), p.159, quoted in Elizabeth Frolet, 'Mingei: The Word and the Movement',

Nihon Mingeikan, *Mingei: Masterpieces of Japanese Folkcraft* (Tokyo, New York and London: Kōdansha International 1991), p.11.

5. Yanagi Sōetsu, adapted by Bernard Leach, *The Unknown Craftsman: A Japanese Insight into Beauty* (Tokyo, New York and San Francisco: Kōdansha International, 1989 edition), p.105, 108, 197, 117, 166, 167.

6. Ibid., p.103

7. See Brian Morean, op.cit., p.23.

8. The term 'floating world', or *ukiyo* in Japanese, was originally a Buddhist concept denoting the sadness of the transience of life. In the Edo period it came instead to denote the thrill of modern life and the excitement to be found in the ephemeral.

9. For examples of such work, see Oliver Impey and Malcolm Fairley (eds.), *Meiji No Takara: Treasures of Imperial Japan* (The Nassar K. Khalili

Collection of Japanese Art); 5 vols, London: Kibo Foundation, 1995.

10. See, for example, Nick Pearce, 'The Rise of the Mingei Movement' in Nihon Mingeikan, op.cit., p.23.

11. The ideas expressed here derive from a lecture given by Paul Greenhalgh entitled 'The Decline of Decoration', given at the Victoria and Albert Museum on 3 March 1994. In Robert Moes and Amanda Mayer Stinchecum, *Mingei: Japanese Folk Art from the Montgomery Collection* (Alexandria, Virginia: Art Services International 1995), p.30, Moes states, with reference to the connection between the Bauhaus and Yanagi, that the former 'strove *valiantly* against Victorian styles, to replace them with *clean, modern, functional styles*'. [Author's emphasis.]

12. The *shōgun* was the military ruler of Japan. The gift from Iemoci also included ceramics, lacquer and metalwork.

13. V&A Archive, Nominal File *Andrews*.

14. 'Hairy' was a term commonly used to describe the Ainu. The captions for one of the illustrations in Batchelor's books is 'A Hairy Specimen'. Rev. John Batchelor, *The Ainu and their Folklore* (London: Religious Tract Society 1901), p.7. For more on Batchelor see chapter 3, pp 106–8

15. V&A Archive, Nominal File *Leach*. The Museum was offered another Ainu textile in 1983, but by then such material was not part of the collecting policy. See Nominal File *Mellott*.

16. At the time of writing it has not been possible to ascertain any bibliographical information about Langewis. As well as collecting objects for the V&A, Langewis procured items for museums in his native Holland. He apparently started his fieldwork in Japan in 1954, having been asked by Dr C. Nooteboom, the Director of the Museum voor Volkenkunde in Rotterdam, to research old weaving methods. The resulting collection, of about 550 textiles and 200 implements used in resist-dyeing, came to the Rotterdam Museum in 1955 and 1956. In the 1960s Langewis collected Japanese textiles, mostly fragments, for the Dutch Textile Museum at Tilburg. These are now also at Rotterdam. The Museum of Ethnography in Delft also has a collection of about 40 textiles given to them by Langewis. I am grateful to Linda Hanssen of the Museum voor Volkenkunde, Itie van Hout of the Tropenmuseum and Sumru Belger Krody of the Textile Museum in Washington for providing this information.

17. V&A Archive, Nominal File *Langewis*.

18. Ibid.

19. In all, Langewis gave or sold the V&A over 150 garments, *futon* covers and textile samples from mainland Japan and the Ryūkyūan Islands. The Indian and South-East Asian Department has some Indonesian textiles acquired from Langewis.

20. V&A Archive, Nominal File *Langewis*. Wingfield Digby's arguments persuaded the Director to sanction the purchase and the whole collection was acquired.

21. Wingfield Digby's interests were very broad. As well as writing on a wide range of European and Asian textiles, he also published on British studio pottery: *The Work of the Modern Potter in England* (London: Murray 1952). His own collection is published in Tony Birks and Cornelia Wingfield Digby, *Bernard Leach, Hamada and their Circle from the Wingfield Digby Collection* (Oxford: Phaidon-Christie *c*.1990).

22. V&A Archive, Nominal File *Langewis*. The letter is dated 25 November 1957. The *kasuri* technique is explained in chapter 3, pp 72–85.

23. The majority of these objects were acquired from American dealers. Many of the best collections of Japanese country textiles have been acquired by museums and private individuals in America over the last few decades.

2 | The Context of Cloth

11 Photograph of an Ainu man wearing an *attush* robe. Late 19th century. 14.7 × 10.0.

The *mingei* movement played a crucial role in the preservation of various types of textiles that might otherwise have been overlooked within the increasingly industrialized society of twentieth-century Japan. The objects promoted and collected by Yanagi Sōetsu and his followers were considered important on the grounds that they were part of the everyday life of the masses rather than the exclusive environment of the elite. Yet the way in which these textiles were viewed effectively removed them from their own 'ordinary' world. In order to understand these objects more fully, they need to be reinstated within their own historical and social context.

The growing body of research on the Edo and Meiji periods provides valuable insights into the social and economic changes that took place in Japan during this time, and the way in which textile production was involved in and effected by these changes. However, the majority of the surviving textiles, particularly those in the V&A's collection, date from only the last part of this period. While the power and prestige of Japan's ruling and wealthy elite ensured that many of the textiles they used were carefully preserved, the belief that the textiles of the common people are worthy of preservation is a relatively recent phenomenon. As a result older examples rarely survive. Emphasis on the 'timeless' beauty of these textiles has also meant that many pieces have been collected without much concern for accurate dating. When selling textiles to the V&A Langewis was often able to record the place of manufacture, but information on dating does not seem to have been available to him. One memorandum relating to a group of textiles acquired by the Museum in 1959 notes that 'all the pieces date from a rather indeterminate period of the middle of the 19th century.'[1] As yet there is little evidence to allow for greater precision.

Despite these problems, however, it is still possible to reconstruct something of the textiles' past and to understand more fully their function and meaning within the communities that produced and consumed them. Through variations of construction and patterning, cloth has a great capacity for communication. It is a significant site of personal, social and cultural identity, since indications of status, wealth, gender, religious beliefs and ideological values can be woven into its appearance. Linked to its importance in the social domain is cloth's role as a commodity for exchange or sale. In the Edo and Meiji periods the economic significance of textiles became increasingly important, particularly to rural communities.

Ainu Textiles

The way of life, beliefs and material culture of the Ainu of Hokkaidō were distinct from those of the mainland Japanese. A deeply religious people, the Ainu believed that spir-

its, both good and bad, were present in every part of the natural world. Their many religious rituals were aimed at soliciting favours from the beneficent spirits and keeping the evil ones at bay. The leading roles in these ceremonies were undertaken by men attired in elaborately decorated elm-bark robes (see figs 5 and 11). The Ainu showed great respect to the gods who protected and provided for them. When stripping bark to make elm cloth the Ainu would thank the tree for giving up its 'clothes'. Only bark from one side would be taken, and when the task was complete offerings of grain and tobacco would be made. A strip of bark would then be wrapped around the tree so that it would not lose any more of its 'clothes' in the wind.[2] Religious beliefs of this kind also informed the decoration of the robes. Strong, web-like motifs served to ward off evil spirits and were laid out symmetrically to protect all parts of the body evenly. Decoration was focused on the hem, upper back and front and sleeve openings to prevent evil spirits from entering at vulnerable points.

Similarly decorated robes also protected Ainu men when they were hunting (fig. 12). This detail from a scroll painting shows men hunting a bear in preparation for *iomante*,

the 'bear sending ceremony', which was the Ainu's most important religious ritual. Spirits were believed to visit the world in disguise, the mountain god appearing in the form of a bear. During the ceremony the captured bear would be killed to release the spirit from its animal form and enable it to return to its own world. While this scroll provides valuable information about Ainu costume, it is important to realise that it was painted by a Japanese artist. The Ainu have been subject to domination and discrimination by the Japanese for many centuries, and the Japanese perception of the Ainu as wild barbarians was reinforced by images such as this. The most distinctive element in this scroll is the way in which the eyes of the figures have been painted. Unlike the narrow eyes seen in depictions of themselves, Japanese images of the Ainu showed the white around the iris, which was believed to be a mark of depravity and dishonesty.[3]

Textiles of mainland Japan

Both the production and function of textiles on mainland Japan, although different from that of Ainu textiles, were also related to traditional customs and social structure.

12 *Scenes of the Daily Life of the Ezo*. Detail. Ink on paper. Anonymous, late 19th century. 27.1 × 1791.4. E.1239–1926.

13 *Woman Returning Home at Sunset.* From the series *One Hundred Poems Explained by the Nurse*, by Katsushika Hokusai (1760–1849). Woodblock print, *c*.1835–6. 25.0 × 36.7.
E.1421–1898.

During the Edo period Japan was ruled by the Tokugawa family, successive heads of which assumed the title of *shōgun* (military leader). A strict hierarchy based on Confucian concepts of the natural order of society was imposed by the shogunate. One was born a *samurai*, a farmer, an artisan or a merchant, and this determined one's status throughout life. Each group had a particular role to play in society, was governed by particular legal codes, and had to conform to particular rules of conduct. In terms of law and social custom a person was defined by their membership of, and position within, a family rather than as an individual. The *ie* (household) was the basic unit of society. Personal ambitions were subordinate to the needs of the *ie*, whose overriding concerns were occupation, status within the local community, and the preservation of household property. Work and home life were not physically separated, and women played an important role in the economic activities of the household while male members helped with child rearing.[4] Fig. 13, a rather romantic image of the countryside by Hokusai, shows women wearing indigo-dyed textiles returning from work in the fields while in the village two men await their arrival.

A woman's duties did, however, embrace the majority of domestic chores, which included the making of garments and other textiles. In rural households a woman's weaving and sewing abilities were considered very important. Ensuring a good marriage was socially and economically vital, and the production of textiles provided tangible evidence of the skills of a potential bride. Such skills were passed from mother to daughter and were also acquired through attendance at the *ohariya* (needle shops). Established in each village, and only open during the winter, the *ohariya* would be run by a particularly skilled farm wife who would teach sewing and other practical skills. From the age of fourteen until marriage young women attended *ohariya* or *musume yado* (girls' rooms), which had a similar function. In some regions a girl was not considered a respectable, marriageable adult until she had attended one of these institutions for some years.[5]

The everyday garments sewn by the women of peasant families do not usually survive in museum collections. Evidence of such clothing can be seen in photographs such

14 Photograph of peasant children. Late 19th – early 20th century. 15.0 × 10.6.

15 Bedding cover (*futonji*).
Cotton with freehand paste-
resist decoration (*tsutsugaki*).
Katanose, Ukiha-gun (Fukuoka
Prefecture), late 19th century.
147.3 × 143.2.
T.332–1960.

as fig. 14, taken at the turn of the century for sale to the expanding number of tourists eager for a lasting memento of their visit to Japan. These often showed picturesquely posed children wearing ubiquitous blue and white garments. As well as serving every-day clothing needs, however, textiles also played an important role in the elaborate cer-emonies that took place in Japan during the Edo and Meiji periods. It is textiles of this kind that tend to be preserved. These special events marked the changing of the sea-sons and important stages of life, such as birth, marriage and death. The textiles used were designed to be noticed, their bold decoration drawing attention to the importance of the ceremonial event.

Many surviving country textiles are associated with weddings. In nineteenth-century Japan the presentation of wedding gifts was an important means by which the family of a bride could establish, in the most public and visual way, their status within the community. It was important for her acceptance in her new home and the pride of her family that a bride be accompanied by a trousseau of impressive wedding gifts. Parents provided their daughters with as many gifts as they could afford. These would include wooden chests, *kimono*, bedding and other textiles. Once the arrangement of a wedding had been agreed, the bride-to-be and other female members of her household would spin the yarn and weave the cloth for the textiles. Decoration of the cloth was generally achieved by dyeing. This was a very specialist skill and, although some dyeing was done in the home, cloth was usually taken to the village dye shop. The importance of wedding textiles would certainly have required the expert skill of the local dyer. While weaving and sewing were done by women, dyeing was usually a male occupation. The choice of designs would depend on the family's taste as well as their wealth. The final sewing of the textiles would be done in the home, and the whole process could take as long as six months to complete. On the wedding day the gifts would be carried in pro-cession to the husband's home.[6]

One of the most important items in a wedding trousseau was the *futonji* (*futon* cover), an example of which is shown in fig. 15. The *futon* is the traditional form of Japanese bedding. When they were first introduced, probably in the seventeenth century, *futon* brought previously unimaginable comfort to the peasant classes, who had been used to sleeping on straw on the floor covered only by the clothes they had worn during the day. The term *futon* refers both to the *shiki-buton*, the mattress spread on the floor, and the *kake-buton*, the cover under which one slept. Both parts of the *futon* were stuffed with raw cotton and would be folded up during the day. It was usually only the top part that had a decorated cover. These covers came in varying widths and were made up of panels of cloth usually twelve to thirteen inches wide. A celebratory *futonji* would be used by a couple on their wedding night. After that it would be treated with great care and used only for special guests.

The *yogi* is another form of bed cover which also featured strongly in wedding trousseaus. *Yogi* are shaped like *kimono* and probably developed from the custom of using robes as bed covers. An extra panel in the centre of the back makes them larger than a *kimono*, however. The *yogi* would cover the sleeper who, for extra warmth, could put his or her arms in the sleeves. A triangular gusset under the arm of the *yogi* allowed for extra movement. Unlike many *yogi* that survive, the example illustrated in fig. 16 still has its cotton stuffing.

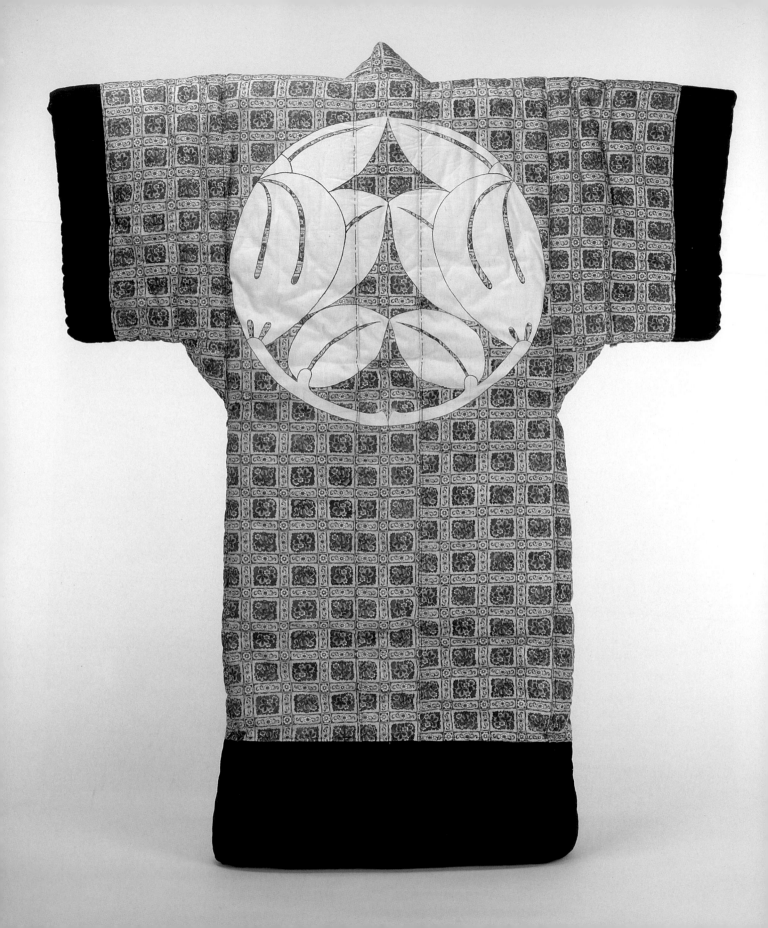

During a wedding procession the gifts would be carried in *furoshiki* (fig. 17). These are square pieces of cloth of varying size for wrapping and carrying objects. Used instead of boxes or bags in the Edo period, *furoshiki* are still prevalent in Japan today. They are lightweight, fold up when not in use and can be wrapped around almost anything, the tied ends serving as a handle. Guests at a wedding would receive a small gift, often of food, which would be wrapped in a *furoshiki*. Another textile bridal gift was the *yutan* (fig. 18). These were intended to cover and protect important gifts, such as wooden chests, and were made specifically to size. As they are constructed in the same way it is often difficult to tell whether surviving textiles are *futonji*, *yutan* or *furoshiki*.

Celebratory textiles were decorated with auspicious motifs deriving from religious or popular beliefs.[7] The designs were chosen to bestow good fortune on the couple. Pine, bamboo and plum were popular motifs, used in combination with each other and with other motifs (see fig. 15). As symbols of longevity, perserverance and renewal they were particularly appropriate for wedding textiles. The pine tree lives for many years

16 Sleeping coverlet (*yogi*). Cotton with printed and paste-resist decoration; cotton wadding. Sakai (Osaka Prefecture), 19th century. 190.0 × 176.0. FE.155–1983.

17 Wrapping cloth (*furoshiki*). Cotton with freehand paste-resist decoration (*tsutsugaki*). Yonezawa (Yamagata Prefecture), late 19th century. 106.5 × 97.0. T.333–1960.

and remains green all the year round. It is also believed to be the dwelling place of the gods. The bamboo is a symbol of resilience, for although it bends in the wind it never breaks. The plum is the first tree to blossom each year and is a symbol of renewal. It is also admired for its flowers, which are said to grow more beautiful as the tree ages.

The decoration on these textiles often takes the form of one image that dramatically fills the whole surface (see fig. 15). Decorative effect was also achieved by the use of repeated and alternating motifs (fig. 19).[8] In this panel of fabric, which was probably once part of a *futonji*, the motif of a pine alternates with that of a crane. Cranes are, like pine trees, symbols of longevity and are believed to live for a thousand years. They are also said to inhabit *Hōrai*, the land of the immortals. In folk stories the crane sometimes features as the heroine who, disguised as a mortal, serves as a beautiful and dutiful wife. Cranes mate for life and the female is extremely protective of its young. Both the real and legendary qualities of these birds made them ideal motifs for wedding textiles. Another kind of pictorial effect was achieved through the combination of a variety of circular motifs. In fig. 20 a butterfly, symbolic of elegance and grace, is combined with plum blossoms and a crane. The crane takes the form of folded paper in reference to the practice of hanging up long strings of *origami* cranes on festive occasions.

18 Bedding cover (*futonji*) or covering cloth (*yutan*). Cotton with freehand paste-resist decoration (*tsutsugaki*). Kyoto, late 19th century. 158.0 × 124.0. T.330–1960.

19 Length of fabric. Detail. Cotton woven with selectively resist-dyed yarns (*kasuri*). Kurayoshi (Tottori Prefecture), late 19th century. 144.0 × 33.0. T.98–1957.

20 Length of fabric. Cotton with freehand paste-resist decoration (*tsutsugaki*). Kyoto, late 19th century. 142.0 × 32.0. T.132–1968.

21 Bedding cover (*futonji*).
Cotton with freehand paste-
resist decoration (*tsutsugaki*).
Late 19th – early 20th century.
146.0 × 130.5.
FE.71–1984.

22 Bedding cover (*futonji*) or
wrapping cloth (*furoshiki*),
detail. Cotton with freehand
paste-resist decoration
(*tsutsugaki*). Late 19th century.
162.5 × 132.0.
T.200–1964.

The mythical *hōō* bird also features on celebratory Japanese textiles, as in fig. 21.
Although it is usually called a phoenix in English, it bears little relation to its western
namesake. In East Asia the phoenix represents peace and prosperity, and is said to
appear only at the time of a truly virtuous ruler. As such the phoenix was often used on
objects displayed in the residences of the military elite. However, it was also a popular
motif among the lower echelons of society. The phoenix is the female counterpart of the
dragon and its many coloured feathers represent the virtues of truthfulness, propriety,
righteousness, benevolence and sincerity, and was thus an appropriate motif for use on
wedding textiles. The phoenix is generally depicted with a paulownia tree which,
according to legend, is the only plant on which the bird will alight. Paulownia wood is
prized for the making of small items of furniture, musical instruments and other
objects. It grows very fast, and it was once the custom to plant a paulownia tree when a
daughter was born so that the wood could be used to make her wedding chest.

Another commonly found combination of motifs is that of the *karashishi* (Chinese

23 Fragment. Cotton woven with selectively resist-dyed yarns (*kasuri*). Late 19th century. 34.2 × 31.5. Circ. 251–1961.

lion) and peony, seen in fig. 22. Chinese culture has always had an important influence on that of Japan and, like many traditional motifs, the mythical *karashishi* is derived from Chinese legend. The lion and peony motif also relates to a Japanese classical play entitled *Shakkyō (The Stone Bridge)*, which tells the story of the monk Jakushō and his visit to Mount Seiryō in China. During the play a lion appears and dances among the peonies to celebrate long life and happiness. The lion symbolizes male energy, while the peony represents female beauty and sexuality. It was therefore an appropriate symbol to celebrate the joining of a man and a woman.

Popular gods and deities also feature among textile motifs. The Seven Gods of Good Fortune were popular household gods deriving from a mixture of Buddhist, Taoist and Shintō sources. Daikoku is the god of wealth. He is usually shown wearing a large floppy hat, part of the imaginary costume of a prosperous Chinese merchant. He is often depicted standing on two bales of rice and carrying a large treasure bag, although in the design shown in fig. 23 only his large smiling face is featured.

Inanimate objects are also depicted on celebratory textiles. Fig. 18 features a bundle of dried abalone strips, or *noshi*. This motif derives from a play on words. A homophone – a word with the same sound as another – of *noshi* means 'extend'. Strips of abalone were traditionally attached to gifts to extend good fortune, and the motif is used on this design as a wish for prolonged happiness. The abalone strips are tied with an ornamental knot, another symbol of congratulations.

The shell-matching game is depicted on the textile in fig. 24. This was played with a set of clam shells. Identical pictures were painted on the inside of each pair of shells, the purpose of the game being to match up the pairs. The imagery was an auspicious one for a wedding couple. This piece of fabric has been mounted as a scroll. It was customary for country textiles to be used and reused in various ways until they were completely worn out, but it is doubtful that highly prized celebratory textiles would have been reused in this way. Indeed, a number of examples in the V&A have been carefully patched (see fig. 51). It is possible that worn textiles were cut up and mounted as scrolls that could be displayed in the home on special occasions, but it is more likely that pieces of fabric were mounted during the mid-twentieth century by dealers who were conscious of the growing popularity of textiles of this kind among collectors. The piece of fabric in fig. 25 has also been mounted as a scroll. The motif of a ship's anchor symbolizes the desire for stability in a bride's new life, also reflecting the hope that she

24 Length mounted as a hanging scroll. Cotton with freehand paste-resist decoration (*tsutsugaki*). Early 20th century. 195.0 × 36.0 (scroll), 115.0 × 32.5 (textile). T.212–1964.

25 Fragment mounted as a hanging scroll. Cotton with freehand paste-resist decoration (*tsutsugaki*). Late 19th – early 20th century. 158.5 × 42.0 (scroll), 43.4 x 30.0 (textile). T.213–1964.

remain 'anchored' in her new home, that the marriage is a success. The anchor image is also used in Izumo, on the Japan Sea coast of western Honshu, on nappies given by a child's maternal grandparents. Here the motif was symbolic of longevity, of 'anchoring' one's life.[9]

Mon (family crests) feature on many celebratory textiles (see figs 15 and 17). Their use was supposedly restricted to *samurai* families, but had spread to commoners by the mid Edo period. *Kabuki* actors and courtesans had made them fashionable, and their popularity soon spread to rural areas. *Mon* served to distinguish one family from another and their display was a means of affirming family status, kinship and loyalty. As if to stress the importance of familial virtues the crests on celebratory textiles are very large and often form the focus of the whole design.

Particular garments were also worn to celebrate special occasions. *Maiwai*, which means 'a thousand congratulations', was the name given to the robes worn by fishermen along the coast of the *Bōsō* peninsula near Edo (see fig. 2). Made from the late Edo period until the Second World War, *maiwai* were worn on New Year's Day or on other special occasions. A symbol of status, they were originally worn only by a ship's owner or captain, but by the beginning of the twentieth century it had become a custom to give them to crews as a bonus for bringing in large catches. *Maiwai* are decorated with colourful sea motifs and auspicious symbols. This example shows two of the Seven Gods of Good Fortune in their treasure ship. The character on the sail is *takara* or 'treasure'. The figure at the back is Daikoku, here complete with sack, while Ebisu, god of daily food and of fishermen, sits at the front. Above the boat flies a crane carrying a banner bearing the name of the ship. The celebratory nature of the robe is also emphasized by its shape: the wide sleeves would have made it an impracticable garment to wear while working.

The unusual and colourful jacket shown in fig. 26 would probably have been worn on a festive occasion. The design is of a *samurai* helmet and arrows, with a *karashishi* among peonies. Motifs featuring warrior accoutrements are usually associated with the Boys Festival, which takes place on the fifth day of the fifth lunar month. On this day a male child's future manhood is celebrated. Given its size this jacket would, however, have been worn by an adult.

Ryūkyūan Textiles

The design and decoration of the striking robe in fig. 27 signify that its owner was of a completely different social status from those who wore and used the textiles described so far. The robe comes from Okinawa, the main island of the Ryūkyū archipelago, which stretches 800 miles between Kyūshū, the southernmost island of Japan, and Taiwan. The first royal dynasty of Ryūkyū was established in 1187 by King Shunten. In 1372 the first official tribute was made to the Chinese Ming court, although trade between the islands and China is thought to have existed before this time. This tribute included textiles, which were to become a major item of trade for the Kingdom of Ryūkyū (united by King Shō Hashi in 1429). The fifteenth century was the dawn of a golden age for the island kingdom, which became one of the most important trading powers in Asia. Goods brought to the islands included silk from China, exotic textiles from South-East Asia, and dyes and trade goods from Korea and Japan. While the

26 Jacket. Cotton with freehand paste-resist decoration (*tsutsugaki*). Early 20th century. 76.0 × 62.0. FE.103–1982.

Detail of fig. 2.

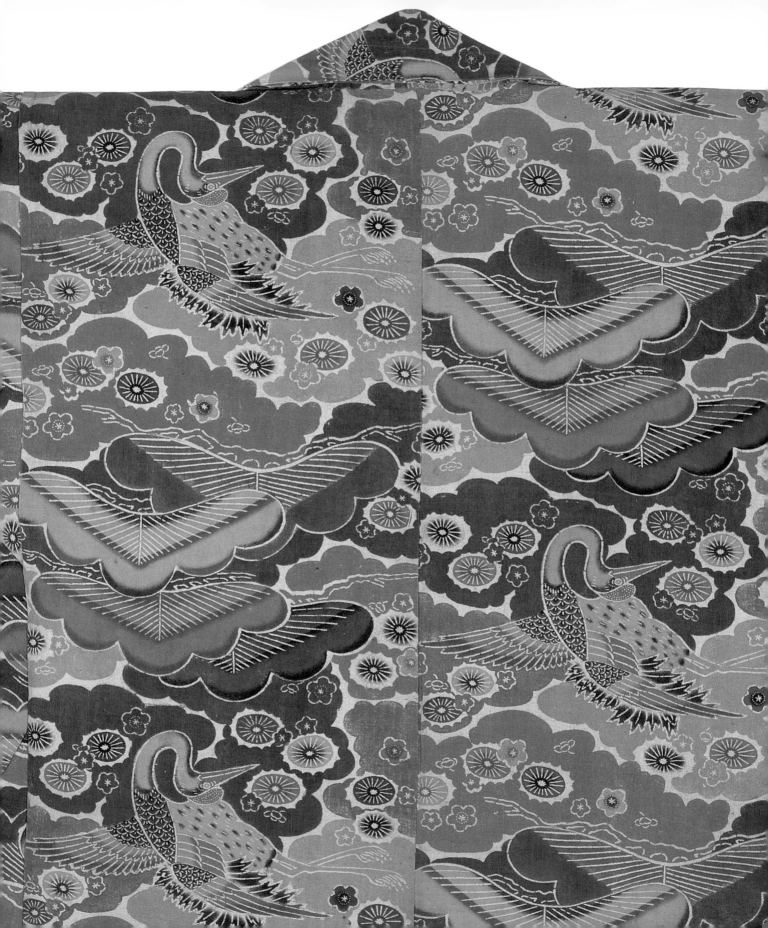

27 Lined robe. Cotton with stencilled decoration (*bingata*). Shuri, Okinawa, Ryūkyū Islands, 19th century.
132.0 × 128.0.
T.18–1963.

influence of Ryūkyū's neighbours can be seen in many of its textile products, the islands also have their own distinctive religious, social and artistic traditions. Their unique fabrics, whether produced for trade, tribute or for the islanders' own use, were, and indeed still are, intimately related to their cultural and political identity.

The forms and colours of *bingata*, the most striking Ryūkyūan cloth, were believed to be imbued with spiritual power. Until the abolition of the aristocracy in 1879 this fabric was reserved exclusively for the use of the Ryūkyūan court. The royal family lived in Shuri castle, Shuri being the Ryūkyūan capital. This was a world from which the common populace were excluded and one from which members of the royal household rarely ventured. *Bingata* was made to order in the Shuri workshops, the dyers themselves being granted the status of lower gentry.

Ryūkyūan garments such as the example in fig. 27 are cut in a similar way to Japanese *kimono*, but are wider and shorter. Unlike *kimono* from the mainland, the sleeves of Ryūkyūan robes are sewn completely to the body of the garment, the sleeve ends are open from top to bottom and there is a gusset under the arm. *Bingata* robes are often lined with fabric of a different design, this being rolled over to form a neckband that stands out in greater contrast to the body, as can be seen in fig. 28. The neckband is also much longer than on Japanese *kimono*. After the islands were annexed by Japan in 1879 the shape of Ryūkyūan robes was generally modified to conform with the construction of garments on the mainland.

Bingata robes were worn primarily by women of the royal family and by court entertainers. Wives of senior members of the nobility were also permitted to wear *bingata* robes on special occasions. Unlike men, women of the nobility did not wear sashes with their robes. The garment would be folded across the body as usual but would be secured by tucking it in at the waist under the unseen tie that secured the undergarment. High-ranking children also wore *bingata*. Particularly brilliant were the large-scale patterns found on the robes worn by the king's sons before their coming of age. The sleeves of these robes were long and, unlike other Ryūkyūan garments, were not sewn to the body. This allowed for a sash to be worn.[10] The child's robe in fig. 29 may have been worn by a boy of the royal family. The curve of the sleeve and the fact that there is only a small armhole would normally indicate that the robe was made after the abolition of the Ryūkyūan royalty in 1879 when the restrictions on who could wear *bingata* were relaxed. The garment has been altered, however, so may date to before that time. The sleeves were originally square, but have been rather clumsily modified. The excess fabric is gathered inside, the original seam being left uncut.

The complex system of fabrics worn at court was introduced from China. Rank was signified by the colour and design of *bingata* garments, both of which were closely regulated. Dragon and phoenix motifs were reserved for the royal family, and the colour yellow restricted to royalty or high nobility. The upper nobility also wore costumes with grounds of white and pale blue (fig. 30). Large-scale designs indicated higher status (see fig. 27), small-scale designs lower status (see fig. 28). *Bingata* was not the only fabric worn exclusively by royalty. Various types of woven fabric were also used. The beautiful example shown in fig. 31, of a fabric known as *hanakuro-ori*, is influenced by Chinese techniques and would have been part of a summer costume worn by a female member of the royal family. Fabric of this kind was produced in very small

28 Lined robe. Cotton with stencilled decoration (*bingata*). Shuri, Okinawa, Ryūkyū Islands, 19th century. 126.0 × 124.0. T.295–1960.

29 Child's robe with modified sleeves. Bast fibre (*asa*) with stencilled decoration (*bingata*). Shuri, Okinawa, Ryūkyū Islands, late 19th century. 88.0 × 86.4.
T.21–1963.

30 Fragment. Cotton with stencilled decoration (*bingata*). Shuri, Okinawa, Ryūkyū Islands, 19th century. 26.0 × 34.0.
T.116–1957.

31 Fragment mounted in an album. Silk. Shuri, Okinawa, Ryūkyū Islands, 19th century. 8.8 × 13.5.
T.142.1–1968.

32 Unlined robe. Striped fibre-banana (*bashō*). Ryūkyū Islands, late 19th – early 20th century. 121.5 × 113.0. FE.12–1985.

quantities. The only surviving garment made from this very elite fabric is in the Japanese Folk Craft Museum.[11]

It was not only within the walls of Shuri castle that clothing was closely regulated. Such rules applied across the kingdom, although most of the documentary evidence that remains is concerned with the nobility. We know that this social group wore *bashōfu* (banana fibre cloth) and ramie in the summer, and silk or cotton in the winter.[12] Garments made out of banana fibre were worn by all classes of society, although the quality of the cloth and the designs that decorated it varied according to status. The striped robe in fig. 32 would probably have been worn by a commoner. It is still of fairly fine quality, however, and is unlikely to have belonged to a member of the poorer peasant class. As with other textiles it is the finest examples, not the most common, that tend to survive. The sleeve construction suggests that it dates from after 1879.

Much earlier in its history, in April 1609, Ryūkyū was invaded by Shimuzu Iehisa, *daimyō* (military ruler) of Satsuma Province. Although the kingdom remained nominally independent until its annexation in 1879, it had effectively become a vassal state of Satsuma and was forced to pay tribute. In order to pay Satsuma, the government in Shuri levied taxes on its subjects, which on the islands of Kume, Miyako and Yaeyama took the form of a poll tax on men and women between the ages of fifteen and fifty, regardless of health or wealth. This tax was known as *nintōzei*. Originally it was a rice tax, but soon after its instigation a portion of it was converted to a cloth tax. Cloth was easier to transport than rice, and also provided good profits for Shuri and Satsuma. In general the rice tax was levied on men, the cloth tax on women, so much of the economic burden of villages on these islands was born by the women. On Kume the tax cloth was paid in the form of *tsumugi*, the silk remaining after fine quality yarn has been removed from the silkworm's cocoon (fig. 48 is an example). On the outer islands of Miyako and Yaeyama it was paid in ramie, especially the finer type known as *jofū* (see fig. 47). *Bashōfu* does not appear ever to have been levied as a tax.

The government at Shuri laid down strict rules about what type, quality, colour and pattern of cloth should be woven. The production of yarn, weaving and dyeing was supervized by local officials, who took their instructions from written guidelines or from *miezuchō* (books containing painted designs). Not all the cloth went to Satsuma, and the boldness of some of the designs suggests that a proportion of the textiles was destined for the Ryūkyūan nobility. Despite the end of royal rule in 1879, the poll tax was not abolished until 1903.[13]

Textiles and the Economy

While no nationwide tax of this kind was ever levied on rural textile producers on mainland Japan, the economic role played by cloth was no less important. The politics of the Tokugawa shogunate, and the social and cultural developments in the large cities, affected the manufacture of textiles even in the most remote areas of the countryside. The demands of the urban markets and the merchants who dominated them were as influential to the creation of these textiles as was the need for peasant farmers to clothe their families.

The unification of Japan by Tokugawa Ieyasu in 1615, and the unprecedented peace and prosperity that followed, encouraged the growth of towns and cities. The power

33 *Naruni: Famous Arimatsu Cloth*. From the series *The Fifty-Three Stations of the Tōkaidō*. By Andō Hiroshige (1797–1856). Woodblock print, *c*.1830–1834. 24.5 × 27.3. E.3756–1886.

and authority of the *daimyō* of each province was centred on the castle towns, some of which were newly created. Former temple or port towns also developed to serve the *daimyō* and their *samurai* retainers as regional centres of craft production and trade. The manufacture of high-quality crafts was still centred on Kyoto, the old capital of Japan and the seat of the Emperor. Osaka, near Kyoto, grew into Japan's major commercial and trading centre. The greatest growth was seen in Edo, the new capital of the shōgunate, which by 1720 had become one of the largest cities in the world with over a million inhabitants.

The growth of cities and towns was facilitated by, and in turn fostered, the development of an extensive trade network. An enormous quantity of goods, both foodstuffs and craft products, was transported to the great markets of Edo, Osaka and Kyoto. Trade between the different provinces also flourished. This network brought great economic and social changes to rural Japan. By the late eighteenth century even the most isolated areas had access to goods produced in other parts of the country. As well as goods, large numbers of people travelled along the expanding highways, a vogue for travel developing among the merchant and artisan classes during the eighteenth century (as depicted in fig. 54). The most famous route was the *Tōkaidō*, the road that linked Edo and Kyoto. The fifty-three posting stations along the *Tōkaidō* became a popular subject for nineteenth-century artists such as Hiroshige (fig. 33). Each station became known for its particular characteristics and for the local products that could be bought there. This print shows Narumi, which was famous for its cloth. Each part of the country had, and indeed still has, its famous *meibutsu* (local product). The *daimyō* encouraged the development of these products as a means of generating extra income, while the rivalry between the provinces ensured the protection of the monopoly of these goods.[14] Travellers often bought these goods, such as the cloth from Narumi, as souvenirs of their travels.

In terms of textile production the most dramatic social and economic changes were brought about by the introduction of cotton. Initially imported from Korea and China, cotton was a fabric worn primarily by the *samurai* class, although there were never any restrictions on its use as there was with silk. It was not until the sixteenth century that it began to be cultivated successfully in the more southerly and westerly areas of Japan. The qualities of cotton were exceptional compared to those of hemp, wisteria and other fibres that up until that point had been the only ones available to the commoner classes.[15] It is impossible to exaggerate the impact cotton had on their lives and the hitherto unimaginable luxury it allowed. Cotton was soft, pliable and comfortable to wear against the skin. Work clothes made of it were strong and durable (see fig. 1) and raw cotton could be used as wadding in winter garments and bedding to give extra warmth and comfort (see fig. 16). In areas unfavourable to cotton production raw cotton was purchased and transformed locally into cotton thread and cloth. Thus even remote agricultural areas were able to enjoy the benefits of cotton, and by the mid-eighteenth century it had become part of everyday life throughout Japan.

The processing of cotton is relatively easy and the farming families who grew it were able to harvest, gin, spin and weave it in their own homes. Throughout the seventeenth century cotton rapidly gained in popularity in the cities and the country. Because of the increased demand farmers were able to sell cotton as a cash crop, and many turned their land over to the cultivation of this profitable plant. It was a risky business however, being dependent on good weather, and prices fluctuated quite widely. Cotton farmers could become very wealthy, but they could also be forced to sell their land and become tenants of richer landowners. Long-established social hierarchies in rural villages were often broken down as the successful production of cotton became the guarantee of status and wealth.

Cotton production was centred on the fertile Kinai region around Osaka. Some farmers carried out the whole process from growing to weaving, but this was generally for household consumption. The majority of cotton that was sold to a wider market took the form of harvested cotton seed. Trade was monopolized by Osaka merchants who controlled the processing and marketing of cotton. In the seventeenth century the greatest demand for cotton fabric came from urban consumers, and the cloth sold to them tended to be produced by urban rather than rural artisans. In the eighteenth century, however, processing began to be undertaken by rural cultivators. New tools for ginning and improved looms for weaving increased productivity. Cotton processing provided an important source of income for the poorer members of village communities. Weaving skills became a marketable commodity, and in some areas men took up activities that had previously only been undertaken by women. The cotton industry also provided richer villagers further opportunities to increase their wealth. Many did not engage in agriculture at all, but acted as petty-capitalists employing wage labour.

The cotton industry became divorced from the actual cultivation of the crop, and the various parts of the processing were split up and managed separately. Some villages specialized in one stage of production, others in several. By 1843 in Uda-Otsu village, near Osaka, only fourteen per cent of the inhabitants were engaged in agricultural production, while forty-six per cent were involved in the cotton industry.[16]

Inroads also began to be made into the monopoly on the trade in cotton goods held by urban merchants such as those in Osaka. During the eighteenth century the Osaka merchants were forced to petition the government on several occasions in order to preserve this monopoly. In 1823 large-scale opposition to the Osaka merchants from over one thousand villages in the Settsu and Kawachi provinces forced the government to end restrictions, which led to a great increase in the rural cotton trade. In the Kinai region the control of the Osaka merchants was replaced by a proliferation of small-scale rural trading groups and independent traders. Cotton production and trade also spread to other areas of Japan, and direct long-distance trade and sales by rural merchants became common.[17]

Textiles and Politics

The cultivation and processing of cotton brought a new and powerful money economy to rural Japan, and encouraged the integration of cotton-producing areas into the ever broadening market system of the country. Initially farmers had begun to cultivate cotton to profit from metropolitan consumption. By the nineteenth century they were actively competing with urban artisans and merchants in the production and supply of finished goods. The ideal of the Tokugawa class system, in which farmers, artisans and merchants were officially separated, no longer reflected the social reality. Although the official settlement of 1823 permitted the increase in rural trade in the Kinai region, the government was concerned by the effect this might have on the social status quo. An order issued by the Osaka City Magistrates in 1842 reveals this unease, stating that 'people from rural areas around Osaka have been adopting urban manners, forgetting their occupations as cultivators, and engaging in commerce...many of them have been acting like cotton merchants and becoming wealthy'.[18]

The strict ordering of society was fundamental to the structure and power of the Tokugawa regime. The blurring of social distinctions caused by the changing social and economic conditions was of grave concern to the shogunate. In order to maintain the distinctions between the social classes, the government issued sumptuary laws regulating the consumption of luxury goods.[19] These were first promulgated in the mid-seventeenth century, and increased in frequency and level of detail throughout the next two centuries. Since clothing was one of the most visible signifiers of wealth and status, it was often the main focus of the sumptuary laws. The wearing of particular fabrics and colours, and the use of certain decorative techniques, were restricted according to social class. Ordinary farmers were not permitted to wear silk even though they might cultivate, spin and weave it. Instead they could dress only in cotton or ramie. *Tsumugi* could be worn by the headman of the village, but only on formal or festive occasions. Certain patterning techniques and colours were also restricted.

The sumptuary laws were also aimed at the townspeople, whose behaviour was of particular concern to the shogunate. It was this social group, particularly the mer-

34 *Fireworks at Ryōgoku Bridge.* By Utagawa Toyokuni
(1769–1825). Six sheet woodblock print,
*c.*1820–1825. 72.6 × 72.6.
E.4900–1886.

chants, who benefitted most from the peace and prosperity of the Edo period, both from the increased demand for goods and the introduction of a cash economy. Many merchants, particularly those who dealt in rice, became extremely rich, but the strict social hierarchy of Edo-period Japan prevented them from using their wealth to improve their official status or gain political power. The strength afforded to the merchants by their economic ascendancy was directed towards the expansion of business activities. The merchants also channelled their money into the pursuit of pleasure and the acquisition of luxury goods, particularly clothes. In the sophisticated urban centres fashion became an important indicator of material wealth and aesthetic sensibilities. The flaunting of affluence by such townspeople worried the shogunate and other social commentators such as Ishida Baigan, who noted in his *Essay on Household Management* of 1744 that:

> Ostentatious people of the present world not only wear fine clothes themselves, but dress their maids in clothing made of thin damask and figured satin with embroidery and appliqué...Lowly townsmen who are so ostentatious are criminals who violate moral principles...They put in disorder the propriety of noble and humble, or honoured and despised.[20]

Anxieties such as these led the shogunate to legislate against excess, aiming to ensure appropriate class display and behaviour.

Country Textiles in the City

The frequency with which the sumptuary laws were reissued suggests that they were not always easy to enforce. The history of urban dress in the Edo period tended to fluctuate between opulence and restraint. When the edicts were more strictly enforced at the end of the eighteenth century there was a shift towards more restrained taste and the use of subdued colours and patterns. It was at this time that the indigo-dyed cotton cloth associated with rural Japan became particularly popular in urban areas. A woodblock print by Toyokuni from the 1820s (fig. 34) shows crowds gathered around Ryōgoku bridge in Edo. Many of the figures wear indigo-dyed textiles, particularly those with a criss-cross pattern in white achieved through the use of a technique called *kasuri*.[21] Since its widespread introduction cotton had been worn by many of the urban lower classes and, as we have seen, this demand helped the considerable growth of the cotton industry in rural areas. The government edicts restricting the clothing of the townspeople meant that indigo-dyed cottons began to be worn by those whose wealth had formerly allowed them to wear fine silks and extravagant embroidery.

The use of such 'lowly' fabrics and patterns did not signify the humble compliance of the merchant classes, however. The gorgeous ostentation denied them was consciously rejected in favour of a new fashion aesthetic known as *iki*, which can be roughly translated as chic. Outward flamboyance was replaced by a subtle elegance, and in prints of the period elegant and fashionable women are often depicted wearing indigo-dyed *kimono* as in fig. 35. The *kasuri* fabrics sold in the cities would have been woven on rural farms by women. The use of this cloth as a saleable commodity and as an indicator of fashion, personal taste and sensibility is a long way from Yanagi's myth of the anonymous rural craftsman making and wearing cloth purely for practical reasons.

Detail of fig. 34.

35 *Girl standing at her toilet.* From the series *Summer Customs of Fashionable Beauties.* By Kikukawa Eizan (1787–1867). Woodblock print, *c.*1815. 38.5 × 26.0. E.3777–1953.

One can see from some of the figures wearing *kasuri*-dyed *kimono* in fig. 34 – for example the woman standing four from the left on the bridge and the man further along holding a fan – that the kind of fabric worn is very fine and almost transparent. The fabric represented is probably not cotton but ramie, of the kind made in Echigo. Despite its geographic isolation Echigo, a mountainous area by the Japan Sea coast, became well known for its fabric, which was sold in Edo, Osaka and Kyoto. The ramie cloth produced there was extremely fine, a quality that is very apparent in the *kimono* in fig. 36. Making the cloth was difficult and time-consuming, and involved the highly specialized skills of many different men and women. It was woven by women working under contract to a producer who supplied the yarn. Echigo cloth was so expensive that the women could not afford to wear it themselves. All of it was sold to the cities where it was worn by wealthy merchants and *samurai*. Although the government edicts placed no restrictions on its use, this was not a humble cloth worn by the common people.

Another cloth associated with the elite is that made from *kuzu* fibre. This is taken from the inner bark of the *kuzu* plant, which was not cultivated but gathered in the wild. It required a great deal of processing to make it pliable enough to weave. Unlike similar fibres that were used in rural areas solely to make work clothes and sacking, the stiff glossy *kuzu* cloth was used for the formal attire of *samurai*. The jacket in fig. 37 is part of the ceremonial costume of a *samurai* fireman, known as a *kajibanten*. Brigades of firemen were assigned to the provincial castles and to the Edo mansions of the *daimyō*,

36 *Kimono*. Bast fibre (*asa*) woven with selectively resist-dyed yarns (*kasuri*). Echigo Province (Niigata Prefecture), late 19th century – early 20th century. 139.0 × 131.0.
FE.52–1982.

37 *Samurai* jacket (*kajibanten*) and chest protector (*muneate*). *Kuzu* fibre. Kakegawa (Shizuoka prefecture), 18th – early 19th century. 83.0 × 124.0.
FE.27–1984.

38 Fireman's jacket. Cotton with freehand resist-dyed decoration (*tsutsugaki*) and quilted in cotton thread (*sashiko*). Late 19th – early 20th century. 95.0 × 122.0.
FE.107–1982.

39 Fireman's hood. Cotton with freehand resist-dyed decoration (*tsutsugaki*) and quilted in cotton thread (*sashiko*). Late 19th – early 20th century. 42.5 × 31.5.
FE.107A–1982.

whose family crests appeared prominently on the costumes. This *kajibanten* would have been worn in the summer, the openwork nature of *kuzu* cloth being particularly suitable for hot weather. At other times of the year a cotton version of the costume would have been worn.[22] These delicate garments were used for ceremonial purposes only. When actually fighting a fire a much more robust jacket, often made of leather, was worn.

The jacket and hood of figs 38 and 39 would have been worn during a fire, but by a townsman fireman rather than a *samurai*. Fires were common in the wooden towns and cities of Edo-period Japan. The capital itself was devastated on a number of occasions. In 1629 Tokugawa Iemitsu created the first fire brigade to protect Edo castle. *Daimyō* and *samurai* brigades were organized thereafter, but it was not until 1720 that a system of townsmen fire fighters was formed to protect the dwellings of the ordinary populace of the city. Fire fighting was extremely hazardous. Before tackling a blaze the fireman would belt his jacket and pull down the flaps of his hood. Wearing these garments, along with trousers and gloves, he would be drenched in water to protect him from the flames. The jacket and hood were made from several layers of thick cotton, quilted together to allow them to absorb as much water as possible. Wearing the heavy cos-

40 Bedding cover (*futonji*).
Cotton with freehand resist-
dyed decoration (*tsutsugaki*).
Late 19th century. 218.0 × 151.0.
T.199–1964.

tume the fireman would use a pole with a hook on the end to pull down the burning
building and thus prevent the fire from spreading. Firemen's jackets are reversible, the
more decorated side usually being worn on the inside. The jackets were made to order
in city workshops and the designs would have been chosen by the firemen according to
their personal taste. This particular jacket is decorated with the dynamic image of a
dragon. This magical and powerful beast, which brought storms when it descended
from the heavens, would symbolically wrap the fireman, bringing him divine protec-

tion as he fought the fire. After successfully defeating the blaze, and on festival days, the jacket would be reversed to reveal the striking design. The courage and reckless action for which Edo townsmen fire fighters were known made them popular local heroes.

While this fire fighter's costume is very much associated with the urban environment, in many cases it is very difficult to know whether a textile was made in the country or the city, particularly as the trade in cloth and finished textiles was so extensive. Certainly the range of textiles produced in the country was more limited. While a village might only have one dye shop, large cities would have many, producing different textiles to suit the needs and purses of a variety of consumers. It is not really possible, or even desirable, to try to drawn a line between what are called 'country' and other types of textiles. The decorative *futonji* so associated with rural wedding celebrations were, for example, also used in the city by the lower classes. It is hard to determine whether or not the family who commissioned the richly decorated *futonji* in fig. 40 lived in a rural or urban area. The pattern of overlapping roundels with various motifs is also found on fashionable silk *kimono* of the period.[23] We know from Langewis's records that some of the textiles he acquired were from Kyoto (see examples in figs 18 and 20).

One textile sighted everywhere in Japan in the Edo and Meiji periods, and indeed still today, is the *noren* (doorway curtain). Commercial establishments were identified by these curtains, hanging in front of their entrances. *Noren* have

41 Doorway curtain (*noren*). Cotton with freehand resist-dyed decoration (*tsutsugaki*). Late 19th – early 20th century. 145.0 × 98.0.
FE.50–1982.

simple but striking designs which suit their function as advertisements. The crest seen in fig. 41 is a common motif, and the name of the shopkeeper, *Ikome*, is also featured in the design. *Noren* are made from separate panels of fabric sewn together at the top. They prevent dust and rain from coming in to the shop, give shade in the sun, stop people peering inside and yet can easily be brushed aside by a customer entering the shop. Symbolically a noren also defines a boundary which visitors are invited to cross. *Noren* would have been one of the most familiar visual symbols of the busy commercial worlds of Edo, Osaka and Kyoto.

NOTES

1. V&A Archive, Nominal File *Langewis*. The memo is from Wingfield Digby to the Director and is dated 26 November 1959.

2. For information on this and other aspects of Ainu textile production, see Michiyo Morioka, 'Ainu Textiles', in William Jay Rathbun (ed.) *Beyond the Tanabata Bridge: Traditional Japanese Textiles* (New York: Thames and Hudson, in association with the Seattle Art Museum, 1993), pp 94–105.

3. Emiko Ohnuki-Tierney, 'The Japanese Representation of the Ainu as seen in the Ainu-e', lecture given at the Meiji Studies Conference held at Harvard University, 6–8 May 1994.

4. Kathleen S. Uno, 'Women and Changes in the Household Division of Labour', in Gail Lee Bernstein (ed.), *Recreating Japanese Women 1600–1945* (Berkeley and Los Angeles: University of California Press 1991), pp 17–41.

5. Anne Walthall, 'The Life Cycle of Farm Women in Tokugawa Japan', in Bernstein, ibid., pp 45–6.

6. For a fuller description of a wedding procession, see Reiko Mochinaga Brandon, *Country Textiles of Japan: The Art of Tsutsugaki* (New York and Tokyo: Weatherhill 1986), pp 11–12.

7. The motifs used in country textiles are discussed in the majority of the books on the subject. Particularly useful is Brandon, ibid., pp 21–8.

8. This is seen particularly in *kasuri* textiles. For an explanation of this technique, see chapter 3, pp 72–85.

9. Brandon, op.cit., p.16 and Michiyo Morioka and William Jay Rathbun, 'Tsutsugaki and Katazome' in Rathbun, op.cit., p.165, footnote 14.

10. This is in contrast to the mainland where long sleeves were worn exclusively by young women.

11. See Sosei Ōshiro and Kanemasa Ashime (eds.), *Okinawa Bijitsu Zenshū* (The Art of Okinawa), vol 3, *Senshoku* (Textiles) (Okinawa: Okinawa Times 1989), plate 78.

12. For a discussion of these fibres, see chapter 3, pp 66–70.

13. For a detailed analysis of this tax, see Amanda Mayer Stinchecum, 'Textile Production under the Poll Tax System in Ryūkyū', *Textile Museum Journal*, 1988–89, pp 57–65.

14. See chapter 3, p. 89 for the monopoly over stencil production held by the Kii Tokugawa family in Shiroko and Jike.

15. For more details on the introduction of cotton, see chapter 3, pp 69–70.

16. Satoru Nakamura, 'The Development of Rural Industry' in Chie Nakane and Shinzaburo Ōishi, *Tokugawa Japan: The Social and Economic Antecedents of Modern Japan* (Tokyo: University of Tokyo Press 1991), p.89.

17. William Hauser, 'The Diffusion of Cotton Processing and Trade in the Kinai Region in Tokugawa Japan', *Journal of Asian Studies*, vol 33, part 4, 1974, pp 633–49.

18. Ibid., pp 645–6.

19. Donald H. Shiveley, 'Sumptuary Regulation and Status in Early Tokugawa Japan', *Harvard Journal of Asiatic Studies*, vol 25, 1964–5, pp 123–64.

20. Quoted in ibid., p.158.

21. See chapter 3, pp 72–85.

22. The V&A has the matching cotton jacket, museum number FE.26–1984.

23. The V&A has a green satin *kimono* dating from the mid-nineteenth century which is decorated with embroidered roundels of flowers. See J.V.Earle (ed.), *Japanese Art and Design* (London: Victoria and Albert Museum 1986), p.90.

3 | Textile Techniques

42 Fragments of cloth. Striped and checked cotton and silk (V,Q), cotton (E,F). Tamba district (Hyōgo Prefecture), 19th century.
162.3 × 32.8, 24.0 × 33.8, 18.5 × 35.5, 17.2 × 33.7.
T.100 V, Q, E & F – 1969.

The many dyeing, weaving and stitching skills which developed in Japan in the Edo period created a rich resource on which people of all levels of society could draw. Designs ranged from the simple to the highly sophisticated, granting the rural and urban lower classes the means to enrich their lives with bold and colourful – as well as practical and durable – garments and household items.

Fibres and Dyes

The fibres and dyes used to weave and pattern country textiles were all obtained from the local environment. Even when the rural producers began to specialize in particular aspects of textile manufacture, the use of local materials remained prevalent. The fine fabrics worn by Japan's military and monetary elites were woven from silk cultivated by farmers, but the latter were prohibited both legally and economically from wearing such luxurious cloth themselves. The peasant classes were permitted to wear *tsumugi* silk, however (fig. 42). *Tsumugi* is the cloth woven from silk obtained from wild cocoons, or from the spoiled leftovers of cultivated silk production. Weaving *tsumugi* was a frugal way of using waste materials and yet producing a warm and soft material. Irregularities in the yarn result in a nubble-textured fabric.

Many of the textiles used by the rural classes were made from fibres gathered from various wild plants. These included *kōzo* and *kaji*, from the paper mulberry tree family, and the vines *fuji* (wisteria) and *kuzu*. The fibres were obtained from the phloem, the tissue that conducts the sap, located in the inner bark of the stems of dicotyledon plants.[1] Processing these fibres was a difficult and time-consuming job. They were very stiff and could not be spun, so they had to be split and joined end to end by tying or twisting. The cloth woven from these fibres was very strong and durable, but coarse and uncomfortable to wear. It was not a particularly good insulator and several layers had to be worn in the winter. The harshness of the weather was commonly described in terms of these textiles, a particularly cold season being called a 'winter of three layers'.[2] Before the widespread cultivation of cotton, however, these fibres were all that were available to many living in rural areas, and a variety of clothing and utilitarian textiles was produced from them. The brown colour of the fibres did not yield to available bleaching methods and the resulting cloth retained its natural hue. The majority of this cloth was worn only by the peasantry, but *kuzu*, as we have seen, did have a more exclusive and specialist use (see fig. 37). As so often with so-called country textiles it is the best, not the commonplace, that survives. The ceremonial costume is the only example in the V&A's collection of cloth made from these fibres. In Hokkaidō the Ainu used fibres from the

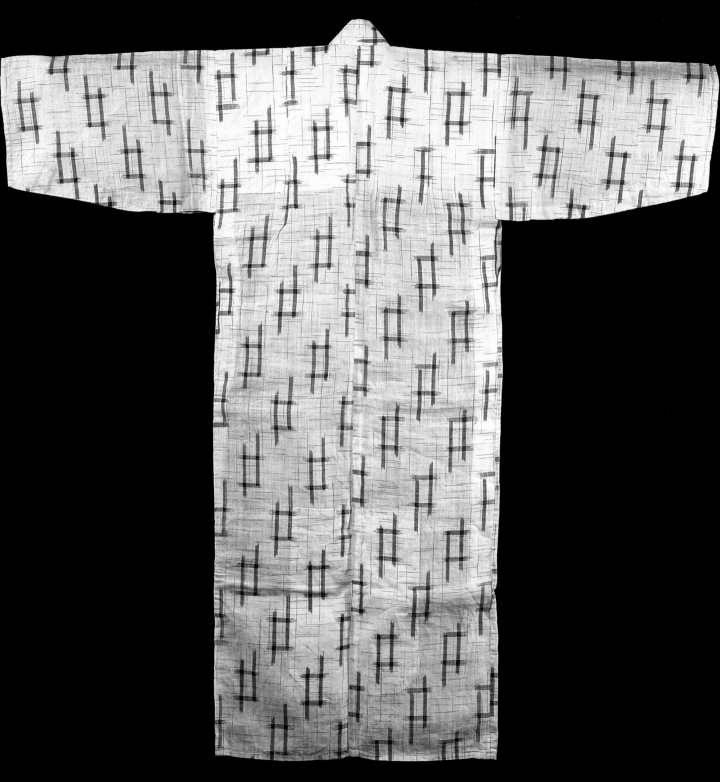

bark of trees such as *shinanoki* (linden) and, most commonly, *ohyō* (elm) which was used to make the *attush* robes (see fig. 5).

Fibres extracted from plants are often known as 'bast fibres'. This term also includes fibres taken from grasses such as ramie and hemp (used in fig. 43). Unlike those obtained from trees and vines growing in the wild, grass fibres were produced from specially cultivated plants. Known collectively in Japan as *asa*, grass fibres could be lightly spun or twisted in a continuous thread and were easier to weave than other bast fibres. *Asa* cloth was also softer than that made from other fibres, and was an important marketable commodity. Ramie in particular could be bleached to produce a lustrous white fabric, and very fine ramie, known as *jofū*, was a luxury cloth used by the military and wealthy merchant classes for summer garments. It was also possible to dye and pattern *asa* cloth in a variety of ways (see figs 3, 43 and 52).

Echigo and Ōmi were two areas particularly famed for producing fine quality ramie. As we have seen, indigo-dyed fabric from Echigo was much prized in urban areas (see fig. 36). Ōmi ramie was a popular everyday fabric in Kyoto as it was produced in the adjacent province. Cloth from Ōmi was commonly dyed white on blue, but brown on white was also used. The fabric for the child's *kimono* in fig. 43 may have come from there. The production of cloth in the province was co-ordinated by merchants based in the highway town of Takamiya. They bought raw *asa* from the mountainous areas in the east of the province, distributing it first to women specialists who spun it, then to dyers, and finally to weavers. Various grades of Takamiya cloth were used by all classes of people, including *samurai*, urban merchants and farmers.

Ramie is also indigenous to the Ryūkyū Islands. The southernmost islands of Miyako and Yaeyama were the main centres for cultivation and production of ramie cloth (see example in fig. 47) which was worn by all classes of society. Only the aristocracy was able to wear the finest grade of the fabric, however. From the late fourteenth century, ramie cloth was sent as a tribute to the Ming court in China. Fine and coarse quality ramie was also levied from Miyako and Yaeyama under the poll tax system introduced after the invasion by Satsuma in 1609.

One cloth unique to the Ryūkyū Islands is *bashōfu*.[3] The fibre used to make this cloth is obtained from the leaf, rather than the stem, of the thread-banana plant. The stalk of the plant consists of concentric layers of leaf sheaths. The long fibres on the outer surface of each sheath are used for weaving. The quality of fibre was best on the innermost layers, and these were used to produce the finest cloth worn on formal occasions. Everyday garments were made from the next layers, work clothes from the next, and cord and rope from the three outermost layers. *Bashōfu* was worn at all levels of Ryūkyūan society. Members of the nobility wore fine quality *bashōfu* in the summer, the stiffness and porosity of the cloth making it especially suitable for the hot, humid weather. Commoners wore *bashōfu* all year round. High quality *bashōfu* was also sent as a tribute item to China. The patterning of *bashōfu* varied according to the social status of the wearer. Commoners wore plain weave cloth patterned with red or brown stripes (see fig. 32), while the royal family wore cloth dyed in bright shades of yellow, red, blue and green. The *bashōfu* worn by members of the aristocracy was often woven with pre-dyed yarns (see fig. 45).

Cotton is the fabric most associated with Japanese country textiles. Most of the coun-

43 Child's *kimono* with modified sleeves. Bast fibre (*asa*) woven with selectively resist-dyed yarns (*kasuri*). 19th century. 108.8 × 110.7. FE.26–1982.

try textiles that survive date from the nineteenth century, so it is easy to forget that this fabric has not always been available to all. Cotton was originally domesticated in the Indus valley of South-East Asia in about 2000 BC, but its spread across the rest of Asia was relatively slow. The earliest surviving piece of imported cotton fabric preserved in Japan dates from the seventh century. The first recorded attempt to actually grow cotton in Japan comes in 799 when, according to a passage in the *Nihon Kōki (Chronology of Japanese History)*, a young man speaking Chinese arrived in Japan with cotton seeds.[4] Attempts to grow the cotton failed, however. Cotton was imported from China and Korea in considerable quantities in the fourteenth and fifteenth centuries, and it was not until the sixteenth century that a species of cotton suitable for Japan's soil and climate was successfully introduced. Cotton was much softer, warmer and more comfortable to wear than cloth woven from bast fibres, and its use transformed the clothing and household textiles of the common populace. The widespread trade in cotton meant that it replaced the use of tree and vine bast fibres, even in areas where it was not locally cultivated. In the poorest and most remote areas, however, bast fibres were still used. More luxurious fibres such as ramie also continued to be cultivated. In the Ryūkyū Islands commoners were permitted to wear cotton in the winter, but here too it remained something of a luxury and most people wore *bashōfu* all year round.

The colouring of cloth is achieved by the use of dyes and pigments. Dyes are soluble in water and penetrate the fibres of the fabric, while pigments are insoluble and adhere to the surface. On the whole dyes are extracted from vegetable sources and pigments derive from minerals. Pigments can also be created from vegetable dyes. The sophisticated dyeing formulas used by urban workshops to decorate luxury fabrics were closely guarded secrets. The dyes used to colour fabrics for the rural classes, however, were easily obtained from common plants. Browns and greys derived from the bark of oak, chestnut and walnut trees. Phellodendron and miscanthus plants produced yellow dyes. Common pigments included *shu* (mercuric sulphide), which produced bright red, *bengara* (iron oxide), which made a red-brown, *ōda* (iron hydroxide) made dull yellow and a bright yellow came from *kiō* or *sekiō* (arsenic trisulphide). Organic pigments were also used, particularly *sumi* (black calligraphy ink), derived from pine soot.[5]

The colour most commonly associated with country textiles is indigo-blue. Although it was introduced to Japan in the fifth or sixth century, its use did not become widespread until much later. The growth in popularity of indigo paralleled that of cotton, the fibre which took the dye most successfully. Hemp and ramie were also dyed with indigo-blue. The indigo-dyeing of *asa* cloth was always undertaken in provincial areas, even if the fabric was destined for the urban consumer.

Ai is the name given to a group of plants containing indican, a water soluble colourless substance that turns blue when exposed to oxygen. While in remote villages women continued to grow their own *ai* and prepare their own dye baths as they had for centuries, the popularity of indigo-dyed cotton in the Edo period meant that dyeing became an independent profession for male artisans. Commercial dye shops were established in cities and villages throughout Japan, and dyeing became one of the most common trades. Indigo preparation and dyeing required great expertise. Most professional dyers did not grow *ai* themselves but purchased it, in the form of a composted concentrate called *sukumo*, from areas specializing in *ai* cultivation. The use of *sukumo* had a number of advantages: it was easy to transport, and made a concentrated dye bath that produced a deep blue colour. Dye baths were considered to have a life of their own and even today dyers treat the bath with great reverence. They are believed to be sacred places, protected by Aizen Myōō, the guardian deity of dyers.[6]

Indigo produced a vivid shade of deep blue when used on cotton and could be applied using a number of different decorative techniques. Repeated dipping in the dye bath built up layers of indigo around the cotton fibres, making them very durable. Indigo could also be combined with other dyes to produce a variety of colours. Green shades, for example, were created by dyeing with yellow over indigo-blue. Indigo was also believed to have medicinal properties. Leaves from indigo plants were used in Japan to treat insect and snakes bites as well as fever and stomach disorders. The wearing of indigo-dyed clothing in the fields was believed to give good protection against snakes and insects, while the depth of the indigo colour concealed dirt and stains. Both practically and aesthetically indigo was the ideal dye, and by the nineteenth century indigo-dyed cotton fabrics were synonymous with rural life in Japan.

Stripes and Checks

The type of weave structure used in the majority of Japanese country textiles is called plain-weave, or tabby, which is the simplest way of interlacing the weft (horizontal) threads with the warp (longitudinal) threads. In this method the weft thread passes over and under each successive warp thread, each row reversing the order of the one before it. The looms used to weave such textiles were also rudimentary. The characteristic feature of these *izaribata* (back strap looms) was that while the back beam holding the warp threads was attached to the wooden frame, the front beam was attached to a strap secured around the body of the weaver. The weaver, most usually a woman, would move her body backwards or forwards to regulate the tension in the warp threads. This method allowed the weaver to loosen the warp to accommodate hand-spun yarns of irregular size or coarse fibres such as hemp. Despite such basic tools and simple plain-weave techniques, great skill and patience were required to achieve a balance of warp and weft, and to maintain the overall tension and subsequent density of the woven fabric. By the nineteenth century the *takahata* (high loom) had replaced the *izaibata* loom in advanced cotton weaving areas. The *takahata* loom had a rigid frame, with the warp threads being stretched between opposite beams. This resulted in a constant tension being maintained during weaving.[7]

Although the weaving methods might have been fairly straightforward, the techniques used to pattern the textiles were often complex and time consuming. Even the most common form of patterning, that of using different coloured yarns to produce striped and checked designs, involved the careful counting of warp and weft threads and relied on the weaver's ability to create a design of overall balance and harmony of colour. Stripes and checks could be used to create an enormous variety of patterns. The examples in fig. 42 come from Tamba, a mountainous region to the northwest of Kyoto famed for textiles of this kind. Cotton was predominantly used to weave these fabrics, but in two of the examples – those that feature blue stripes on a pale ground – silk as well as cotton was used for the weft in order to produce a more varied texture and a softer fabric.

44 Sash (*obi*). Torn strips
of cotton. 19th century.
283.5 × 15.0.
FE.27–1982.

Ryūkyūan *bashōfu* was also commonly patterned with stripes. The rich brown colour of the stripes on the *kimono* in fig. 32 was probably produced using a dye made from the woody part of the *sharinbai* tree, a member of the rose family. The golden colour of the ground is the natural colour of the cloth, which has darkened with age.

Striped effects could also be created by using thinly torn-up strips of cotton cloth taken from garments or other textiles that had become too worn for use. This method is known as *sakiori*, which literally means 'torn weaving'. In the *obi* (sash) in fig. 44, the wefts consist of cotton strips of various colours interspersed with white. The warp threads are of black cotton, and have been left fringed at each end.

Kasuri

In Japan a distinction is made between *sakizome*, meaning textiles produced by the weaving of pre-dyed yarns, and *atozome*, meaning textiles produced by the dyeing of pre-woven textiles. The stripes and checks seen in fig. 42 are example of *sakizome*, as is the technique known as *kasuri*. The softly blurred pattern of white against deep indigo-blue created by this technique was one of the most familiar features of Japanese clothing during the nineteenth and early twentieth century (see fig. 14). The strong association of *kasuri* with the *mingei* aesthetic has, however, obscured the fact that it was used not only to pattern the clothing of farmers, but that of fashionable town dwellers, *samurai* and members of the Ryūkyūan court.

Kasuri is a thread-resist technique. Sections of yarn are tightly bound or compressed prior to being dyed. The dye does not penetrate these protected areas when the skein of yarn is dipped into the dye bath, a process that is repeated a number of times to achieve the required depth of colour. The binding is then carefully removed, leaving a yarn that is partly white and partly coloured. If various colours, or shades of blue, are to be used, the yarns are tied and retied as necessary. The yarn is then used as the warp or weft (or sometimes both) so that a pattern emerges as the cloth is woven. The slight misaligning of the resist-dyed threads gives the patterns on *kasuri* cloth their characteristic blurred outline. Great skill is required of the dyer to bind the threads in exactly the right place to ensure that the pattern will appear as planned.

There are various theories as to the derivation of the word *kasuri*. It may have developed from *kashiri*, which is the term used to describe thread-resist textiles on the Ryūkyūan island of Yaeyama. *Kasuri* is also phonetically similar to words that describe haziness or blurriness.[8] *Kasuri* is synonymous with the word *ikat*, which is used to describe the same technique in Indonesia and Malaysia. As with other technical terms *kasuri* describes the resulting cloth as well as the method used to achieve it. When *kasuri* techniques were first introduced to Japan in the late sixteenth and early seventeenth centuries, methods of thread-resist dyeing were already known. Very early examples of such textiles, imported into Japan from mainland Asia in the eighth and ninth century, are preserved in the Shōsōin Imperial Repository in Nara. In the Heian period (794–1185), thread-resist techniques were used to create flat ceremonial sashes. There are several surviving Muromachi (1393–1568) and Momoyama (1568–1615) period *kimono*, in which changes in background colour have been achieved by reserving large sections of the warp threads. This method continued to be used in the creation of *Nō* theatre costumes in the Edo period (1615–1868). These elite examples are very

different in concept, appearance and function, however, from those textiles known as *kasuri* and the term was never used to describe them.[9]

Japanese *kasuri* is believed to have its roots in the Ryūkyū Islands. In the fourteenth and fifteenth centuries the islands stood at the heart of an extensive maritime trade network, and *ikat* techniques are thought to have been imported from India, South-East Asia and Fujian province in south-east China.[10] The *kasuri* textiles that were subsequently created in Ryūkyū became highly prized at court, and were also important as trade and tribute items. Most of the developments in *kasuri* weaving took place in the southernmost islands of Miyako and Yaeyama. In South-East Asian *ikats*, it is the warp threads that are resist-dyed. This means that once they have been stretched on a loom flexibility of design is not possible. Ryūkyūan weavers, however, began to use resist-dyed yarns for the weft. Because these threads could be manipulated as weaving progressed, more painterly images could be created. What made these developments possible were differences in loom construction. Ryūkyūan looms, unlike those of South-East Asia, use reeds, also known as 'spacers', to separate the warp threads. Once warps did not bunch together it was possible to position the weft threads accurately. It is this use of resist-dyed weft threads that makes Japanese *kasuri* unique. The resist-dyeing of both the warp and the weft creates further decorative possibilities, as patterns can be created in both directions. Independent warp or weft patterns appear as half-tone images when sections of undyed threads cross dyed sections. Where undyed warp and weft threads intersect, sharp, white designs are formed. In Ryūkyūan *kasuri* it is usually

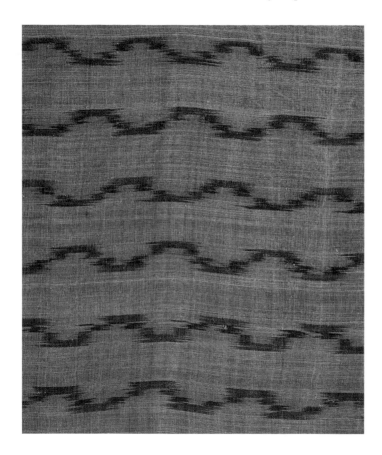

45 Fragment. Fibre-banana (*bashō*) woven with selectively resist-dyed yarns (*kasuri*). Ryūkyū Islands, 19th century. 18.2 × 30.0. T.104.16–1969.

46 Fragment mounted in an album. Silk woven with selectively resist-dyed yarns (*kasuri*). Shuri, Okinawa, Ryūkyū Islands, 19th century. 19.5 × 23.7. T.142.44–1868.

the sections of the yarn that will form the pattern rather than the ground that are dyed (as in fig. 47).

The *kasuri* technique has been used to pattern the example of *bashōfu* cloth seen in fig. 45. Although *bashōfu* was worn by all sections of Ryūkyūan society, only the gentry and aristocracy were permitted to wear *kasuri* patterned garments. Such restrictions were lifted after the abolition of the kingdom in 1879, but such fabrics still tended to be worn by only the upper echelons of society.

One *kasuri* method that is thought to be unique to the Ryūkyūan islands is that of *hikizurashi* (slide pulling). As the resist-dyed threads are woven into the fabric, each weft is shifted to either left or right. In this way oblique or curved motifs can be formed. The piece of fabric shown in fig. 46 is a striking example of the radiant colours often seen in Ryūkyūan *kasuri*. The style of patterning, in which motifs occur in every other square of a lattice, is known in Ryūkyū as *tijima*, and was generally used to pattern robes worn

47 Fragment mounted in an album. Bast fibre (*asa*) woven with selectively resist-dyed yarns (*kasuri*). Miyako or Yaeyama, Ryūkyū Islands, 19th century. 11.5 × 17.8.
T.142.33–1968.

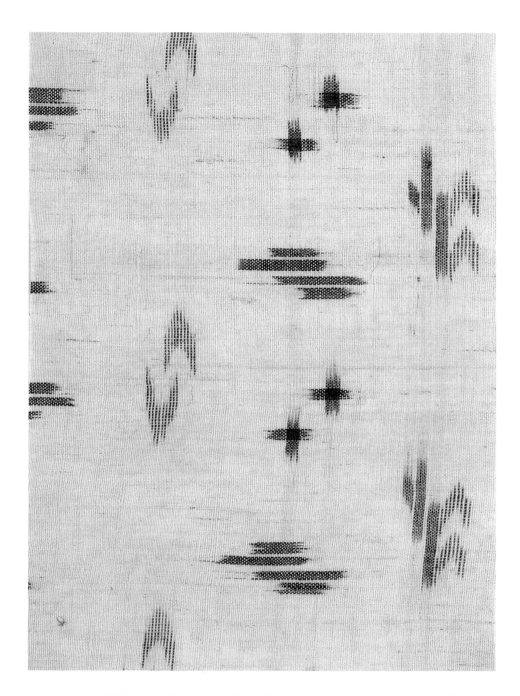

by the young. This example is woven from silk and would have been made in the capital of Shuri. The bright colours and large-scale design suggest that it would have been part of a garment worn by a member of the royal family or a very senior member of the aristocracy.

The introduction of *kasuri* to mainland Japan resulted from Satsuma's invasion of the Ryūkyū Islands in 1609 and the subsequent imposition of poll taxes. In 1636 the tax of rice was replaced by one of textiles in Miyako and Yaeyama. These two islands

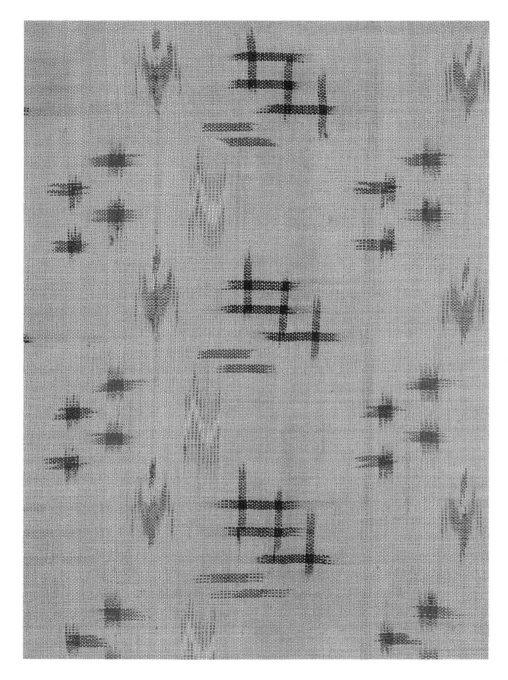

48 Fragment mounted in an album. *Tsumugi* silk woven with selectively resist-dyed yarns (*kasuri*). Kume, Ryūkyū Islands, 19th century. 12.5 × 18.3. T.142.36–1942.

were particularly famous for *kasuri* dyeing and weaving, and the tax may well have reflected the already growing demand for *kasuri* textiles on the mainland. The piece of ramie in fig. 47, with its *kasuri* pattern of blue against a white ground, was probably woven as a tax cloth. It has the quiet design and sense of space for which many Ryūkyūan *kasuri* fabrics were admired. Fig. 48 was probably made on Kume, a small island due west of Okinawa. The bright yellow of the ground contrasts with the elegance of the small-scale motifs. The shade of red, derived from sappanwood, was

49 *Kimono*. Bast fibre (*asa*)
woven with selectively resist-
dyed yarns (*kasuri*). Ojiya
(Niigata prefecture), 19th
century. 133.5 × 122.5.
T.329–1960.

used exclusively on tax cloth.[11] Both these fabrics would have been worn by members
of the military elite on mainland Japan. Until recently, it was assumed that *kasuri* techniques were slowly disseminated from Satsuma to the rest of Japan.[12] However, new
evidence has shown that the pattern of early *kasuri* production on the mainland was
more complex.[13] The *daimyō* took their entire retinues with them when they travelled
to Edo which they were forced to do regularly under the *sankin-kotai* system.[14] Artisans
brought their own technical and artistic knowledge to the capital and returned to their
provinces with newly acquired information. This, and the well-established road and
sea trade routes established in the Edo period (1615–1868), played an important role in
the spread of *kasuri* and explains why the technique appeared in apparently uncon-
nected parts of the country.

   In the geographically isolated Echigo, *kasuri* techniques developed as early as the
1660s as a result of the area's independent trade links with Ryūkyū. It was also
common for farming communities in the area to supplement their income with textile
production during the cold winter months. The cloth was then sold through Osaka, a
city with which Echigo had also established trade connections. Once introduced, *kasuri*
techniques were quickly incorporated into the existing textile repertoire. Sold from the
wholesale markets of Osaka, Echigo cloth reached a wide network of admiring consumers. The area was most famed for the production of cloth with small-scale hatched
kasuri designs as in fig. 36, but other patterns were also created. The *kimono* in fig. 49,

50 Length of fabric. Cotton woven with selectively resist-dyed yarns (*kasuri*). Katanose, Ukiha-gun (Fukuoka Prefecture), late 19th century. 200.0 × 93.5.

T.326–1960.

51 Bedding cover (*futonji*). Cotton woven with selectively resist-dyed yarns (*kasuri*). Katanose, Ukiha-gun (Fukuoka Prefecture), late 19th century. 170.0 × 155.0.

T.325–1960.

52 Length of fabric. Bast fibre
(*asa*) woven with selectively
resist-dyed yarns (*kasuri*).
Kurume (Fukuoka Prefecture),
late 19th century. 140.0 × 33.0.
T.99–1957.

53 Cape. Cotton woven with selectively resist-dyed yarns (*kasuri*). 19th century. 90.5 × each panel approximately 22.0 at hem, 5.5 at neck. FE.1–1988.

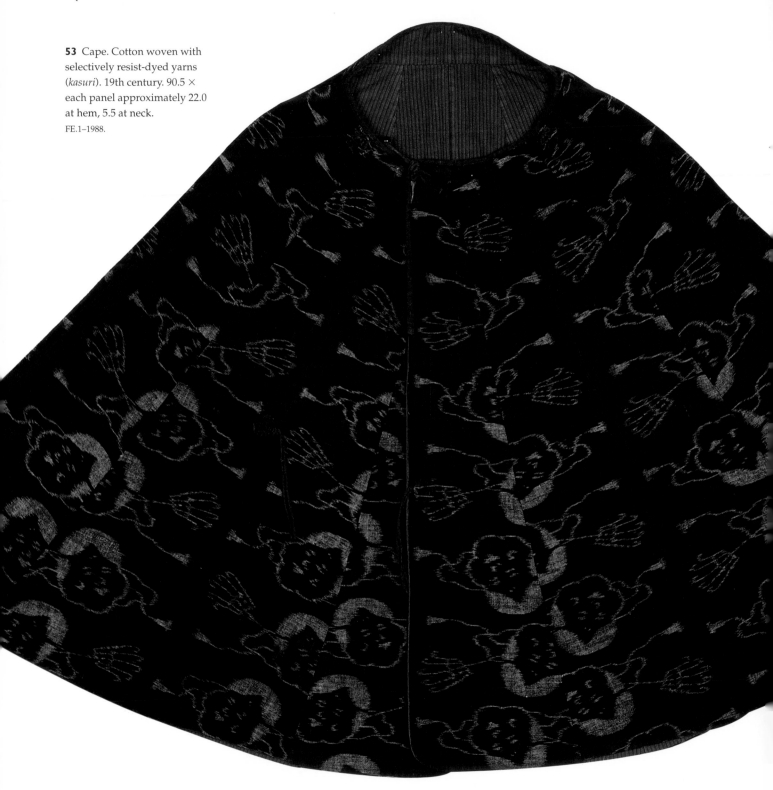

with its decoration of chrysanthemums interspersed with a criss-cross design, was bought by Langewis in Echigo (now Niigata Prefecture).

By the late eighteenth century, *kasuri* weaving was well-established in many parts of Japan. Unlike those of the Ryūkyū Islands, the *kasuri* fabrics of mainland Japan were predominantly indigo-dyed. Among the rural classes the *kasuri* technique was used to pattern household items. The length of fabric in fig. 50 was probably part of a *futon* cover. Diagonal lines formed by small squares alternate with a checkerboard design of squares within squares, in two shades of indigo, to produce a very bold design. One of the most striking characteristics of Japanese *kasuri* is the use of freeform and realistic designs. So-called *e-gasuri* (literally picture *kasuri*) elements are often interspersed with geometric motifs such as on the *futon* cover in fig. 51.

The combination of geometric and pictorial designs was also used to good effect on clothing (see fig. 49). The *kasuri* technique has been employed with great sophistication on the piece of fabric shown in fig. 52. Woven from *asa*, it is probably a *kimono* length rather than part of a *futon* cover, as the latter were made from softer cotton. The background design, of groups of progressively broader stripes, creates the effect of waves over which the fish leap. The simultaneous creation of the two parts of this elegant design required enormous skill on the part of both dyer and weaver.

Fig. 53 is a *bōzugappa* (travel cape), whose style was adapted from capes worn by Portuguese missionaries in the sixteenth century. The word derives from *bōzu* (priest) and *kappa*, the Portuguese for cape. It is circular, and constructed from sixteen gored (triangular) sections

54 *One Hundred Views of Mount Fuji*, vol 1, plate 9. By Katsushika Hokusai (1760–1849). Woodblock printed book, 1835. 22.6 × 15.8 (closed book). E.6724–1916.

55 Fragment. Bast fibre (*asa*) woven with selectively resist-dyed yarns (*kasuri*), the warp yarns hand-tied, the weft yarns board-clamped (*itajime*). Ōmi Province (Shiga Prefecture), mid- to late 19th century. 38.3 × 32.6.
T.106 –1957.

of cotton. The *kasuri* design is of Okame, the goddess of mirth, no doubt chosen to cheer the traveller on his journey. The cape is lined with cotton with narrow blue, black and orange stripes, and has a stand-up collar. The wearing of such capes was originally restricted to members of the military, but by the eighteenth century other sections of Japanese society had adopted it. These garments are often illustrated in woodblock travel prints such as the one by Hokusai shown in fig. 54.

The increasing complexity and size of *kasuri* images was aided by various technical developments in the nineteenth century. These included the *e-dai* (picture stand), which consisted of a frame with bamboo combs at each side. The distance between the combs equalled the length needed to weave one weft row. Cotton thread was wrapped around the frame to create a false weft face. Onto this an image would be painted with the aid of a stencil or a drawing placed under the threads. These threads then acted as a guide for the tying of the actual weft yarn prior to dye immersion. The *kobajōgi* worked in a similar way, using slivers of paulownia wood, each representing a single weft thread, stacked up on edge. A pattern was then painted on, and the numbered pieces of wood would then be used as a guide for the dyeing of the weft threads. Both these methods allowed considerable artistic freedom.

This was also true of the *itajime* technique, which had the additional advantage of speeding up the dyeing process. In this method the yarn was pressed tightly between two boards that were carved with the desired image. Clamped around the fabric, the boards were then immersed in the dye, which would penetrate the carved areas through pierced holes. *Itajime kasuri* is distinguishable by its more clearly delineated images and the bands of white that appear at the selvedge edge as can be seen in fig. 55.

Tsutsugaki

The patterning of cloth after it has been woven can be achieved in a number of ways. In Japan one of the most common methods is that of *norizome* (paste-resist). It is unclear when this technique was first used in Japan, although it may have been as early as the Kamakura period (1185–1392).[15] The use of paste as a resisting agent probably originated in China, where soyabean flour was used. In Japan, however, the paste was made of rice flour, water and lime. Not only was rice a readily available resource, but it proved an excellent base for the paste. Fine patterns could be produced and, being water soluble, the paste could then be easily washed off to leave a sharp-edged design.

One technique that uses rice paste is *tsutsugaki* (tube drawing), which was used on the fabric shown in fig. 56. In this method woven fabric is stretched on a frame of bamboo, and the design drawn onto the cloth with paste squeezed from a *tsutsu* (tube). The tube is fashioned from paper, made water-resistant through treatment with persimmon juice, and the paste is extruded through a nozzle of bamboo or metal. The width of the drawn line depends on the size of the opening of the nozzle. This paste forms a protective coating that prevents the dye penetrating when colour is brushed on or, in the case of indigo-dyeing, the cloth is immersed in the dye vat. Often the paste is applied to both sides of the fabric to ensure a clear, crisp image. Before the dye is applied the entire surface of the cloth is brushed with soyabean liquid to seal the paste and help fix the dye. Once the dyed cloth is dry, it is placed in hot water to soften the rice paste, which is then washed off.[16]

A few *tsutsugaki* patterned garments have survived from the Muromachi period. These examples consist mostly of costumes for the *Nō* theatre and *kimono* for the wealthy, so it seems likely that the use of the technique was originally reserved for the clothing of the elite. By the eighteenth century, however, *tsutsugaki* was used throughout Japan by the peasant classes. Although it required a great amount of skill and was time consuming, *tsutsugaki* afforded a fairly inexpensive way of producing designs for commoners in both town and city. As a free-hand method of drawing, the repertoire of possible images was limited only by the talents of the dyer. The bold and colourful patterns that could be created using this technique were ideally suited to celebratory textiles such as *futonji*, *furoshiki* and festival costumes (see figs 15, 17, 18, 21, 22 and 26).

56 Bedding cover (*futonji*). Cotton with freehand paste-resist decoration (*tsutsugaki*). Hakata (Fukuoka Prefecture), late 19th century. 160.0 × 124.0. T.331–1960.

57 Doorway curtain (*noren*). Cotton with freehand paste-resist decoration (*tsutsugaki*). Early 20th century. 95.5 × 63.0. FE.49–1982.

On the *futonji* in fig. 56, the *tsutsugaki* technique has been used to create a design of chrysanthemums and waves. The pattern would first have been drawn on the cloth with a brush. The paste would then have been squeezed out along the lines. A spatula-like implement would probably have been used to spread the paste over the large areas. The paler shade of blue would have been produced after only a few dippings in the dye bath, and these areas would then have been covered with paste before the cloth was dipped again. The petals of the flowers were probably painted on directly with a brush. This *futonji* is a wonderful example of how subtle shading can be achieved using

only one colour. The *futonji* in fig. 21 with the phoenix design is decorated in various colours which would have been brushed on. Brushed dyes tend to rub off, and so it is likely that this *futonji* would have been far brighter when it was originally made. The lines of paste that would have prevented one colour bleeding into another are left white when the paste is washed off. This integral part of the technique creates a bold outline which adds to the dramatic force of the design. This example also shows how the *tsutsugaki* technique could be used to create large-scale patterns not easily achieved by other dyeing methods.

The boldness of *tsutsugaki* designs made them extremely suitable for use on *noren* (doorway curtains), the visually striking motifs being ideal for the purposes of advertising. Fig. 57, with its octopus design, may have been used on the doorway of a shop or restaurant specializing in seafood.

Katazome

Rice paste can also be applied to fabric through stencils in a technique known as *katazome*, which has been used in fig. 58. The use of stencil decoration in Japan goes back at least as far as the Nara period (646–794). Seventh- and eighth-century examples of paper decorated by spraying pigment through stencils are preserved in the Shōsōin Imperial Repository. In the Kamakura (1185–1336) and Muromachi (1336–1573) periods, the technique of applying colour through stencils was employed to decorate deerskin and other kinds of leather used in armour. It is not known exactly when the method was first used in conjunction with rice paste to decorate textiles, although it is possible that cut-paper stencils were introduced from China in the sixteenth century. One of the earliest styles to emerge was that of *komon*: very small-scale designs that were used throughout the Edo period to pattern the formal attire of the *samurai* and the garments of wealthy townsmen. By the mid Edo period a new variety of larger-scale stencil designs, known as *chūgata*, became popular among all classes and was used on clothes and household items.

During the Edo period the Japanese stencil-cutting industry was concentrated in Shiroko and Jike, two small towns in Ise Province (modern-day Mie Prefecture). Production was stimulated by the powerful Kii Tokugawa family who ruled the province. Through their protection and influence they were able to secure for their artisans and merchants a virtual monopoly of the stencil trade. Stencils are made from two or three sheets of *kōzo* (mulberry) paper laminated together with persimmon juice. In addition to its adhesive qualities, the juice strengthens the paper and makes it water-resistant. Cutting is usually carried out on seven or eight stencils at a time. Various methods and tools are used to create different kinds of patterns – from the small and intricate (as in fig. 59) to the large and bold (as in fig. 60). *Kiribori* (awl cutting) is used to create patterns of small dots; *tsukibori* (thrust cutting) creates dynamic floral, arabesque or scenic designs; *dōgubori* (tool punching) punches out designs; and *hikibori* (pull cutting) creates very fine stripes.[17] Striped patterns, and patterns with large open spaces, are secured with a net of fine silk to prevent distortion when the paste is applied. As stencil patterns repeat across the length of the fabric, careful attention needs to be given to the cutting of the edges of the stencil to ensure perfect matching. Complex patterns often require the use of two stencils, an *omogata* (main stencil) and a *keshigata* (fill-in stencil).

58 Bedding cover (*futonji*), detail. Cotton with stencilled decoration (*katazome*). Late 19th – early 20th century. 144.0 × 121.5. FE.11–1985.

After the paste-resist is applied through the first stencil, a soluable pigment is some-times brushed on to act as a guide for the second stencil, which needs to be aligned pre-cisely in order to create a flawless pattern.

The application of rice paste is carried out with the fabric stretched on long boards. The stencil is placed on the cloth and the rice paste is applied through it with a wooden or bamboo spatula. The stencil is removed and repositioned on the next section of

59 Stencil. Mulberry (*kōzo*) paper. 19th century. 30.4 × 39.5. D.1350–1891.

fabric, the process being repeated along the entire length of fabric. Once the paste is dry, a sizing liquid, normally of soyabean extract, is applied over the entire cloth. When it is to be seen from both sides, the fabric is turned over and the rice paste applied in reverse. This is often done when the cloth is to be immersed in a dye vat, as with indigo, to prevent the dye bleeding into the resisted areas. Shading and extra colours may be added by brush or secondary stencils, either before or after the background is dyed. When the colours are dry, the paste is washed away, leaving the undyed areas to form the pattern against a dark ground (as in fig. 53). Occasionally the design is coloured while the ground remains undyed (as in fig. 61). Fig. 62 is an unusual example of stencilled cloth in which different patterns are used along the length of the fabric. In addition to the indigo, brown and yellow dyes have been brushed on by hand, the latter sometimes in conjunction with the indigo to give a blue-green effect. Customers visiting dye shops may have been shown lengths such as this to help them decide what

60 Stencil. Mulberry (*kōzo*) paper. 19th century. 24.8 × 40.2. D.957–1891.

61 Bedding cover
(*futonji*), detail.
Cotton with stencilled
decoration (*katazome*).
Late 19th to early
20th century.
157.0 × 126.0.
FE.13–1985.

62 Length of fabric.
Bast fibre (*asa*) with
stencilled decoration
(*katazome*).
19th century.
99.4 × 27.0.
T.164–1966.

63 *Girl in the snow.*
By Utagawa Kuniyoshi
(1798–1861).
Woodblock print,
c.1843. 85.5 × 29.0.
E.10550–1886.

kind of pattern they desired. It appears that the use of blocks of different stencil designs was a popular style itself among the urban classes of the nineteenth century.[18] The woodblock print by Kuniyoshi (fig. 63) shows a girl making a snowman. She is wearing a number of indigo-dyed fabrics, including a *kimono* patterned with stencils. This image of a fashionable beauty of the city confirms that techniques such as stencil-dyeing were as much part of the urban as the rural environment.

Bingata

One of the most spectacular uses of stencils can be seen in the *bingata* textiles of Okinawa. *Bingata* means something like 'scarlet patterns' and refers to the multicoloured fabrics associated with the Ryūkyūan royalty. Little is known of the origin of the technique. The method of using paste-resist may have come from China, while the colourful patterns suggest the influence of India and South-East Asia.[19] The entire process,

64 Child's robe with modified sleeves. Cotton with stencilled decoration (*bingata*). Shuri, Okinawa, Ryūkyū Islands, late 19th century. 85.3 × 79.0. T.19–1963.

65 Fragment. Bast fibre (*asa*)
with stencilled decoration
(*bingata*). Shuri, Okinawa,
Ryūkyū Islands, 19th century.
13.0 × 32.5.
T.114–1957.

66 Fragment. *Tsumugi* silk with
stencilled decoration (*bingata*).
Shuri, Okinawa, Ryūkyū
Islands, 19th century.
53.0 × 32.8.
T.117–1957.

from the making of the stencils to the final finishing of the garments, was carried out
within one household workshop. The basic method of stencil-dyeing is similar to that
on mainland Japan. What distinguishes *bingata* is its brilliance of colour. The vivid
palette derives from the use of mineral pigments held in a medium of soyabean liquid.
The pigments are applied with a stubby brush in a number of layers to achieve the
intensity of colour required.[20] While many of the motifs are similar to those of Japan
and China, the colourful decorative style of *bingata* is very different from that of mainland and continental textiles. Some of the garments have extremely dense patterns, as
in fig. 28. Other robes have freer patterns which, although based on repeated pattern
units, give a sense of overall pictorial composition, as can be seen in fig. 64. This rhyth-
mic design, of stylized streams and irises, was particularly favoured by the Ryūkyūan
aristocracy. Although predominantly applied to cotton, *bingata* stencil designs were
used on other fabrics such as ramie (see figs 29 and 65), crêpe-weave silk (fig. 66) and
gauze silk (fig. 67). Silk was often used on *bingata* undergarments such as the plain silk

67 Fragment. Silk with
stencilled decoration (*bingata*).
Shuri, Okinawa, Ryūkyū
Islands, 19th century.
38.2 × 20.4.
T.113–1957.

68 Undergarment (*dujin*). Silk
with stencilled decoration
(*bingata*). Shuri, Okinawa,
Ryūkyū Islands, 19th century.
79.5 × 126.0.
T.20–1963.

example in fig. 68. Such jacket-style undergarments are known in Ryūkyū as *dujin*, and
are held in place by a set of ties on the inside and outside.

Although *bingata* is usually brightly coloured, some fabrics were dyed with indigo
alone. This is known as *aigata* in Japanese, *ye-gata* in Ryūkyūan. In fig. 69 various
shades of indigo-blue against white were used to create a design of flowers and birds.
The ground was covered with paste and the foreground design dyed first. The paste
was then washed from these areas and the fabric re-immersed in the indigo. This dark
blue against light blue is known in Ryūkyūan as *kuru-bana-njashi* (exposing black flowers). Parts of the flowers and the wing-tips of the birds were resisted throughout and

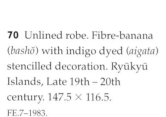

69 Fragment. Cotton with indigo-dyed (*aigata*) stencilled decoration (*bingata*). Shuri, Okinawa, Ryūkyū Islands, 19th century. 71.4 × 34.0.
T.102–1969.

70 Unlined robe. Fibre-banana (*bashō*) with indigo dyed (*aigata*) stencilled decoration. Ryūkyū Islands, Late 19th – 20th century. 147.5 × 116.5.
FE.7–1983.

remained the colour of the undyed fabric, highlighting the otherwise understated design.

On the *bashōfu kimono* in fig. 70 the staggered diamond design, reserved in white on a dark blue ground, was also created using *aigata*. An identical design appears on the reverse of the fabric. Rather than stencilling again on the back, this was probably achieved by brushing the cloth with water and scraping with a knife to draw the paste through. The colour would then have been brushed on to both sides. The elegance of the design and the fineness of the *bashōfu* cloth suggest that this garment would have been worn by a member of the elite.

Sarasa

Rice resist-paste may have developed in Japan as a substitute for the wax used in many parts of India and South-East Asia. During the Edo period Indian and Indonesian textiles were imported into Japan by the Dutch East India Company. These colourful wax-resist or block printed fabrics, called *sarasa* in Japanese, were very popular. At this time the Japanese were not allowed to travel abroard and the Dutch were the only Europeans permitted to trade with Japan. They not only exported Japanese items to Europe, but imported various goods both from the West and from their trading bases in South-East Asia. Such exciting and exotic objects were eagerly sought by the Japanese. The vogue for imported textiles can be seen in Kunisada's woodblock print, fig. 71, in which a courtesan, the epitome of up-to-date fashion, is surrounded by a great swathe of *sarasa* fabric covering a *futon* or *yogi*.

Although more likely to have been imported, it is possible that the fabric depicted by Kunisada was of the kind made in Japan. The woodblock printed book in fig. 72 is entitled *Sarasa Benran*, and was published in 1781. Subsequent editions were published in 1784 and 1808. The book contains designs inspired by imported Indian and Indonesian

71 *Girl writing a letter*. From the series *A Collection of Contemporary Beauties*, by Utagawa Kunisada (1785–1864). Woodblock print, *c*.1815. 38.0 × 26.4. E.8598–1886.

72 *Sarasa Benran*, Vol 1, page 10. By Kusumi Magozaemon Chikari (worked *c*.1750–1800). Woodblock printed book, dated 1781. 26.7 × 16.5 (closed book). E.6924–1916.

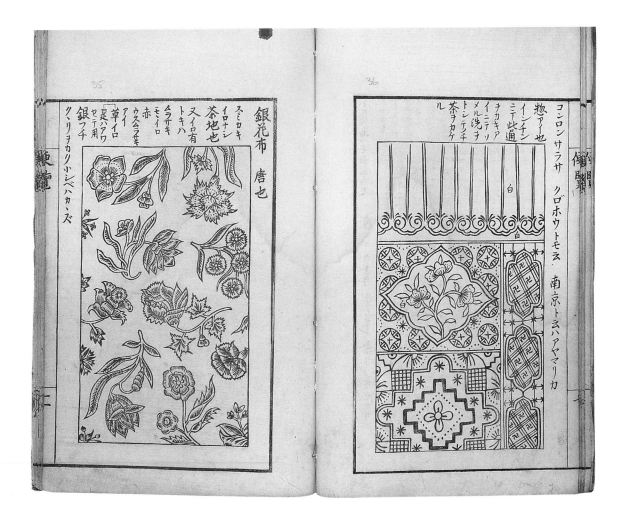

textiles, with notes on suggested colours. The patterns are for *fuki-e* (blown pictures), in which dyes are blown through stencils onto cloth. Many Japanese *sarasa* fabrics were created with stencils, but wax-resist and block printing methods were also used. These various techniques were often used in combination.

As with other textiles, the use of *sarasa* was not exclusive to one section of society. In Saga province high-quality *sarasa* was made to order for the local Nabeshima *daimyō*, but in Nagasaki, Kyoto and Sakai it was produced for use as *futon* covers, *furoshiki* and *yogi* by the lower section of society. The *sarasa yogi* (figs 16 and 73) in the V&A's collection was made in Sakai in the nineteenth century. The small-scale design of checks containing flowers in brown, blue, yellow and green was created using wooden blocks. These would have been carefully carved with the design, then brushed with dye before being stamped onto the fabric. A different block would have been used for each colour. It is possible that some of the areas of colour were applied through stencils.

Appliqué and Embriodery on Ainu Textiles

Although the majority of country textiles are decorated using resist-dyed methods, there are notable exceptions. Designs on Ainu textiles are created exclusively by appliqué or embroidery. As these techniques are similar to the patchwork ones used by

73 Sleeping coverlet (*yogi*), detail. Cotton with printed and paste-resist decoration; cotton wadding. Sakai (Osaka Prefecture), 19th century. 190.0 × 176.0. FE.155–1983.

74 Ainu robe (*attush*), detail. Elm-bark fibre (*ohyō*) with cotton cloth appliqué and cotton thread embroidery. Hokkaidō, mid-19th century. 128.5 × 128.0. T.99–1963.

75 Mat. Elm-bark fibre (*ohyō*) with cotton cloth appliqué and cotton thread embroidery. Hokkaidō, late 19th to early 20th century. 33.0 × 30.0. T.269–1910.

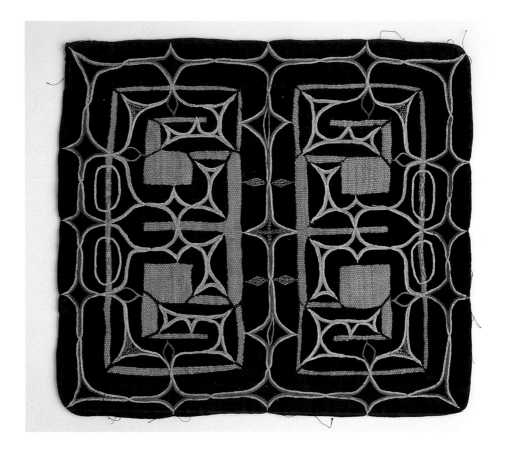

76 Two purses. Elm-bark fibre (*ohyō*) with cotton cloth appliqué and cotton thread embroidery (left). Cotton with cotton thread embroidery (right). Hokkaidō, late 19th to early 20th century. 12.5 × 14.0, 12.5 × 10.0 (when closed). T.270 & 268–1910.

the Ainu to fabricate leather items, they may pre-date woven fabrics. Cloth was woven on a back strap loom which, unlike that used on the mainland, did not have a wooden frame. Instead the warps were anchored to a stable object such as the trunk of a tree or a stick embedded in the ground. The appliqué method used on the robe seen in figs 5 and 74 is known as *kirifuse* (meaning to cut and lay down). Pieces of indigo-dyed cotton cloth, imported from the mainland, have been stitched down in a pre-determined design. This has been embellished with an embroidery technique known as *oki-nui* (placing and sewing), with thick white threads couched down to create the thorn-like motifs.[21] The sleeves and the body of the robe would have been decorated separately, then sewn together.

Similar decoration can be seen on other textiles used by the Ainu. The *ohyō* (elm bark) mat in fig. 75 has been almost totally covered with strips of blue cotton, which have then been embroidered in various colours using chain and stem stitch. No couching has been used on this example, nor on the two purses in fig. 76. The purse on the left has a cotton cloth edging and flap, and on the back blue cotton weft threads have been woven with the *ohyō* to create stripes. The purse on the right is made solely from cotton, the inside lined with red. Skills of appliqué and embroidery were important ones in Ainu society. The nineteenth-century missionary the Reverend Batchelor wrote:

The men take great pride in their wives' needlework, and they are exceedingly particular about having the corners of their ornamental patterns properly turned. If a

curve is not quite so well turned as a man thinks it should be, or a line not quite straight, he will storm away finely and sometimes make his wife unpick her work and do it all over again.[22]

Although Batchelor seems to reduce the decoration of garments to a subject of domestic quarrel observed by a slightly amused outsider, his comments do reveal the importance of these designs and the skills needed to produce them. By the beginning of the twentieth century the traditional way of Ainu life was fast disappearing, and many garments were sold to tourists or made solely for the tourist market. The model robe in fig. 7 was made as a tourist item by an old woman living in the Hakodate Ainu Industrial Home. According to V&A records she told Miss Andrews, who gave the robe to the Museum, 'of her indignation and tearfulness when, a few years ago, she one day returned from her field work to find that her husband had been lured by a passing tourist into selling for fifty shillings the beautiful coat which she had spent four long years embroidering for him'.[23]

Sashiko

Quilting, known as *sashiko*, was a stitching technique used by the mainland Japanese. This method of sewing together one or more layers of cloth with a simple running stitch was initially used as a way of making fabric last longer, or to recycle old pieces of cloth in a new garment. Clothing that was stitched in this way was strong and warm, and thus suitable as working apparel. On the indigo-dyed farmer's coat (shown in figs 1 and 77), three different quilting patterns have been used. The main body has been

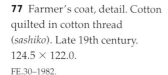

77 Farmer's coat, detail. Cotton quilted in cotton thread (*sashiko*). Late 19th century. 124.5 × 122.0. FE.30–1982.

78 Sledge-hauling jacket. Cotton quilted in cotton thread (*sashiko*). Late 19th century. 83.0 × 46.0. FE.108–1982.

densely stitched with horizontal and vertical running stitches in a diamond pattern. The quilting on the sleeves, which are of a darker fabric, is less tightly spaced and the diamond pattern is more curvilinear. Small, individual diamond shapes are stitched around the neck. Except in the sleeves, the quilting stitches go through both the outer fabric and the lining.

Another instance of the use of *sashiko* to make a garment more durable is seen in the sleeveless jacket in fig. 78. This garment features some of the stitching patterns for which the Shōnai Plain (Yamagata Prefecture) is known. As in the farmer's coat there are three different quilting patterns on the main body: a persimmon flower motif on the shoulders, a diamond pattern in the middle, and a zigzag pattern near the hem. The use of blue thread on a blue ground is known as *kakurezashi* (hidden stitch). As the garment was worn and repeatedly washed, the indigo of the cotton thread would have faded at a different rate from that of the fabric, and thus the quilting patterns would have been gradually revealed. Contrasting with this subtle patterning a band, decorated in white permisson flower stitches, runs diagonally across the body of the jacket. This dramatic feature is related to the use of the garment for hauling sledges. The position of the band and its stitching would have reinforced the fabric against the tension that would have occured when the jacket was in use. The excellent condition of this jacket, however, suggests that it was never actually worn for its intended purpose.

The *sashiko* technique found on the fireman's outfit in fig. 38 is also appropriate to the garment's function. A simple vertical running stitch is used across the entire garment to bind two or three layers of cloth together. These multiple layers protected the fireman, and absorbed the water in which he was drenched before approaching the flames. The decoration on a fireman's garments relies not so much on the *sashiko*, however, as on the design executed in *tsutsugaki*.

Far from the urban environment of the fireman is Tsugaru (Aomori Prefecture), the area of Japan most famous for *sashiko*. This is the most northern part of Honshū, the main island of Japan. In this mountainous and cold area, warm durable clothes were very important. The climate of Tsugaru was not suitable for the cultivation of cotton, however, and cotton cloth for quilting was bought from elsewhere. Locally grown ramie and hemp were woven as the base fabric for *kogin*, a technique that was developed from *sashiko* and used to embellish *kimono* (fig. 79). In *kogin*, white stitches are embroidered over and under an odd number of warps to produce a diamond pattern. The base fabric is usually woven quite loosely to assist the counting of the

79 *Kimono*. Bast fibre (*asa*) with cotton stitch embroidery (*kogin*). Tsugaru district (Aomori Prefecture). Late 19th to early 20th century. 128.0 × 102.5. FE.141–1983.

warp threads. This must be done very precisely to ensure the severe regularity of the pattern. The place of origin of *kogin* textiles is reflected by the patterns, large diamond designs (as in this example) coming from the east of the region. The decorated sections have been stitched separately and then inserted into the garment. If a Tsugaru woman was to ensure a good marriage, it was essential for her to learn the *kogin* technique. Training began at an early age, and by the time of her marriage a woman would have woven and embroidered a number of *kimono* for herself and her husband-to-be. The use of embroidery on these garments was not an indication of harsh living conditions or strenuous work. *Kogin*-decorated *kimono* such as the one in the V&A's collection were special garments to be worn on formal occasions.

NOTES

1. See Louise Cort, 'Bast Fibres' in Rathbun, op.cit., p.38. Cort also describes a number of other bast fibres used in various parts of Japan.

2. See Brandon, op. cit., p.38.

3. See Cort, op.cit., pp 40–41.

4. See Brandon, op.cit., p.39.

5. For information on the plants and minerals used for dyeing in Japan, see Monica Bethe, 'Dyes and Colours' in Amanda Mayer Stinchecum, *Kosede: 16th–19th Century Textiles from the Nomura Collection* (Tokyo and New York: Japan Society and Kodansha International 1984), pp 202–9.

6. For a full description of the history and techniques used in indigo-dyeing, see Brandon, op.cit., pp 43–52.

7. See Brandon, op.cit., pp 41–2.

8. These words include *kasuru* (to graze, abrase or blur); *kasureru*, which denotes the end of a calligraphic brushstroke; *kasumeru* (to brush lightly); and *kasumi*, which refers to mist or haze. See Mary Dusenbury, 'Kasuri' in Rathbun, op.cit., p.59.

9. For a description of these and other examples of Japanese thread-resist methods, see Mary Dusenbury, 'Kasuri: A Japanese Textile', *Textile Museum Journal*, vol.17, 1978, pp.42–7.

10. The evidence as to exactly how and when the *ikat* technique reached the Ryūkyū Islands is still somewhat scant, however. See Amanda Mayer Stinchecum, 'Textiles of Okinawa', Rathbun, op.cit., pp 81–2.

11. For an extremely similar example, see Sosei Ōshiro and Kanemasa Ashime, *Okinawa Bijutsu Zenshū (The Art of Okinawa)*, vol.3 of *Shenshoku (Textiles)*, (Okinawa: Okinawa Times 1989).

12. See, for example, Jaap Langewis, 'Japanese Ikat Textiles', *Kultuurpatronen*, vol. 5/6, 1963, p.77.

13. See Mary Dusenbury, 'Kasuri', *Textile Museum Journal*, vol.17, 1978, p.50–51.

14. *Sankin-kotai* (meaning alternate residence) was introduced by the third Tokugawa *shōgun*, Iemitsu, in 1634–5. Under this system, which was designed to keep the provincial military leaders under control, each *daimyō* was required to maintain a residence in Edo. The *daimyō's* immediate family remained permanently in Edo while he spent every other year in attendance there.

15. This theory derives from the evidence of paintings. See Reiko Mochinaga Brandon, op.cit., p.31.

16. *Tsutsugaki* is very similar to *yūzen*, a technique used on the elegant garments of the urban rich. The colouring of *yūzen* is usually achieved by the brushing on of colours rather than immersion in dye baths. A tube with a very fine nozzle is used to create very sophisticated patterns. Although technically related to *tsutsugaki*, the extreme delicacy of line in *yūzen*, which made it a time-consuming process, and the fact that it was used predominantly on silk, meant that the finished garments were far too expensive for the majority of Japanese.

17. For more details on these techniques, see Rupert Faulkner, *Japanese Stencils* (London: Victoria and Albert Museum 1988), pp.9–10.

18. This information was given to the author by Matsubara Yoshichi, a contemporary textile designer who has studied Edo period stencils at great length. See chapter 4, pp 122–4.

19. For a discussion of the various theories about the origin of *bingata*, see Okamura Kichiemon, 'Bingata, a Historical and Technical Study', in Ōshiro and Ashime, op.cit., pp.100–8.

20. For a list of the pigments used in *bingata*, see Amanda Mayer Stinchecum, 'Textiles of Okinawa', in Rathbun, op.cit., p.82.

21. Couching is the term used to describe the technique of placing threads on the surface of the fabric and attaching them with small stitches.

22. Batchelor, op.cit., pp.148–9.

23. V&A Museum Register: T.264–1910.

4 | Continuity and Change

Japan experienced great social, economic and cultural changes during the Edo period. Rapid urbanization created thriving metropolises and fostered the development of a consumer culture. Improved transportation and communication systems encouraged the evolution of a nationwide market economy. In rural areas there was a substantial growth and diversification of agricultural production, and an increase in manufacturing and commercial activities.

Significant though these developments were, it was during the second half of the nineteenth century that Japan experienced perhaps the most profound changes in its history. In 1853 an American naval squadron arrived in Edo Bay, presenting demands for the opening of ports to foreign ships. A treaty with America was established in 1854 and with other western powers soon after. The disruption that these external pressures caused exacerbated growing internal unrest, culminating in the overthrowing of Tokugawa rule and the restoration of the Meiji Emperor in 1868.

One of the major aims of the new government was the renegotiation of treaties which had effectively been forced on the Japanese, and which signified in their terms the superiority of the western nations over Japan. To compete with the military and industrial might of the West, it was apparant that Japan would have to transform itself along western lines. During the Meiji period a modern industrial economy was built up, and legislative and judicial systems were reformed. Western style buildings were constructed, western style gatherings were organized, and western style dress was adopted by those who embraced the concepts of civilization, modernization and progress that the Meiji government was seeking to promote.[1]

The transformation brought about in the Meiji period affected all aspects of life, but that does not mean that changes occurred immediately or universally. Western customs only slowly permeated the population as a whole, and traditional textiles continued to play an important role in Japanese culture. The work clothes (figs 1, 38 and 78), fine quality *asa kimono* (fig. 36), celebratory textiles (figs 15, 17–25 and 56) and festival garments (figs 2 and 26) that feature in this book all date from the late nineteenth and early twentieth century. Until the 1920s and 1930s, when Japan's programme of industrialization came to fruition, the country remained a basically agrarian society and the majority of the population continued to reside in small rural villages.

While the late nineteenth century was characterized as much by continuity as by change, the making of textiles was fundamentally affected by the replacing of handwoven goods with machine-made ones. When trading with the West began, the importation of inexpensive cotton cloth threatened to damage the domestic cotton industry. The division between processing and manufacturing that was established in the Edo period meant that it was customary for producers of cloth to purchase their thread from elsewhere. Foreign factories were able to supply advanced cotton-producing areas with an abundant supply of cheap, but high quality, thread. These areas were able to compete successfully against imported cloth while self-sufficient cottage industries foundered. Farmers who cultivated cotton and those who processed thread also found themselves deprived of work.

In 1873 Japan imported from France and Austria the 'flying shuttle' loom that had been invented in Lancashire, England, in 1733. By 1877 it was in widespread use throughout the country. Productivity increased greatly and from the 1870s the Japanese cotton industry developed rapidly. A mechanized cotton-spinning industry developed in the 1880s. By 1900 Japan not only had no need of imports, it was actually exporting a third of its cloth to China and Korea.[2] During the Meiji period the textile industry accounted for over sixty per cent of the entire industrial workforce. Eighty per cent of these workers were young women. They brought in extra income for their families and, being paid fifty per cent less than men, provided a cheap labour force for the employer.[3]

The role of bast fibres in textile production was also profoundly changed in the Meiji period, although in a very different way from cotton.[4] The *kuzu* cloth industry, for example, was dependent on the *samurai* who wore garments woven from this fabric on ceremonial occasions (see fig. 37). The abolition of the warrior class thus had disastrous effects. The cloth was adapted, however, first as a cover for *fusuma* (sliding doors) in Japanese houses and then as wallpaper, which was exported to Europe and North America until the 1960s. Korea eventually took over the supply of *kuzu* cloth to western markets, the plant having been introduced there in 1910. Now only a small amount of *kuzu* cloth is woven in Japan, for sale as souvenir 'folk craft' items.

In 1879 the Ryūkyū Islands were annexed to Japan and became Okinawa Prefecture. Restrictions on the types of fabric and patterning that could be worn by different social groups were abolished along with the Ryūkyūan royal family. Commoners developed their own hierarchy, however, with *kasuri* being worn for special occasions, simpler *kasuri* and checks and stripes being used for everyday clothes, and stripes or plain for work garments. The poll tax system did not end until 1903. This system had made ramie textiles well known on the mainland and they continued to be made, becoming important commercial goods. As in the days of the poll tax, the much prized fabric was not worn by those who produced it.

In contrast *bashōfu* was not known on the mainland as it was never used as a tax cloth. With the availability of cheap machine-made cloth, and the increasing popularity of western style garments, the production of *bashōfu* declined rapidly. In the 1930s, however, *bashōfu* came to the attention of Yanagi Sōetsu, who praised it both for being processed totally by hand and for being worn by all classes of society. A few years later the ravages of the Second World War swept over Okinawa. The islands were lost to Japan at the end of the war and remained in American hands until 1972. Although it seemed as if traditional textile practices would be lost forever at this point, *bashōfu* was revived after the war, first under the auspices of the Folk Craft movement and later with the support of the Japanese government. In certain areas there are also producers who remain independent of central government patronage.[5]

Bingata suffered a similar fate. Formerly dependant on royal patronage, *bingata* dyers were forced to seek a popular audience. Commoners were either unable to afford the prized fabric or were reluctant to wear something that had previously been the sole prerogative of royalty. Like *bashōfu*, *bingata* was 'discovered' by Yanagi, although he misinterpreted its historical use. Similarly, *bingata* risked being lost forever after the war, but the technique has been revived by a number of dyers. Traditional Okinawan textiles are no longer made to meet economic or social needs. They survive because of their artistic importance, not merely as echoes of the past, but as signifiers of the islands' desire to establish a cultural identity strong enough to resist the dominance of mainland Japan.

The *bingata* screen in fig. 80 is not by a Ryūkyūan however, but by the Japanese artist Serizawa Keisuke (1895–1984). Serizawa originally trained as a graphic artist rather than as a textile designer. In 1926 he met Yanagi Sōetsu, an event that marked the beginning of his lifelong involvement with the Japanese Folk Craft movement. The turning point in his artistic career came in 1928 when he saw *bingata* fabrics displayed in an exhibition. His enthusiasm led him to travel to Okinawa in the 1930s to study *bingata* stencil-dyeing techniques. During his lifetime Serizawa created a great diversity of stencil-dyed textiles in a wide range of formats including *kimono*, *noren*, book illustrations and screens. In one way this appropriation of an Okinawan technique by a Japanese artist may be viewed as indicative of the submission of the islands to not only political but cultural control by the mainland. Yet as one of the most important and influential textile artists of the twentieth century Serizawa has done much to ensure the continuing survival and appreciation of *bingata*. In this screen he has not used the *bingata* technique to depict a particularly Japanese subject, but has instead created the most direct and powerful image of Okinawan identity possible, a map of the island itself. In vignettes around the map Serizawa has depicted various images of Okinawan life and cultural activity. One of these depicts *bingata* fabrics.

The Japanese Folk Craft movement was born just at the point when the industrialization of Japan was reaching a peak and when many Japanese intellectuals were trying to establish a sense of cultural nationalism in the face of overwhelming western influence. The movement did much to preserve traditional Japanese crafts during this critical period. Yet the objects so admired by Yanagi and his followers were only recognized as having artistic significance on the eve of their disappearance. Indeed *mingei* acquired meaning through its contrast, less with the cultural products of the elite than with mass produced commodities of the machine age. *Mingei* could never be more than an ideal, for the notion of an unselfconscious, anonymous, craftsman producing beautiful utilitarian objects for the masses was no longer tenable, if indeed it ever had been. Objects from the pre-industrial past were viewed with romantic nostalgia because the world in which they were created no longer existed.

In his engagement with contemporary artists Yanagi was successful in inspiring the re-evaluation of traditional craft practices. Yet the success of artists such as Serizawa negated the ideal of anonymity, and ensured that only wealthy connoisseurs were able to buy their work. Serizawa's empathy for his materials and his understanding of techniques were no less profound than those of the unknown makers of the objects so admired by Yanagi. Just as it is necessary to understand these 'folk crafts' within the

80 Six-fold screen. By Serizawa Keisuke (1895–1984). Silk with stencilled decoration (*bingata*). Tokyo, *c*.1940. 170.0 × 183.0. FE.21–1985.

historical context that *mingei* denied them, it is important to be aware of the complexity of issues that surround the activities of twentieth-century makers.

The turmoil of the Second World War caused irrevocable social, economic and cultural changes in Japan. While the concerns of artists and thinkers of the pre-war period still existed, they needed to be addressed within a different framework. The trauma of defeat and occupation by foreign forces stimulated a new surge of interest in Japan's traditional past. This past seemed all the more compelling in the face of the great destruction of buildings that had occurred during the war, and the increasing Americanization of Japanese culture. Japan looked to the past to provide stability and a sense of national identity.

Fears that traditional Japanese buildings, artistic practices and customs were in danger of being lost led the Japanese government to review the laws relating to the protection of cultural properties. New legislation promulgated between 1950 and 1955 covered not only 'tangible cultural properties', such as buildings, but 'intangible cultural properties' as well. The latter were defined as 'intangible cultural products materialized through such human activities as drama, music, dance and the applied arts which have high historical or artistic value'.[6] A nationwide survey was carried out and a list compiled of performing and applied arts felt to be worthy of preservation and in danger of dying out. The scope of the law was extended in 1954 to cover traditional practices not necessarily facing extinction but considered particularly important.

The dyeing and weaving practices designated as Important Intangible Cultural Properties included *bashōfu* from the village of Kijoka on the northern coast of Okinawa island, and fine quality ramie or *jōfu* from Miyako. On the mainland the textile types covered by the new law included *jōfu* from Echigo and Yūki *tsumugi* (shown in fig. 81). The latter is produced in farming areas around Yūki city in Ibaraki Prefecture in eastern-central Japan. The production of the fabric was already flourishing by the fourteenth century, but became very popular in the nearby capital during the Edo period. Yūki *tsumugi* was originally used only for men's garments but in the Meiji period it was increasingly in demand for women's clothing. The V&A's example dates from about 1960. The raw *tsumugi* silk has been spun by hand and woven on a back strap loom. The *kasuri* technique has been used to create a dense zig-zag pattern from yarns that have been resisted in black, brown and blue.

Japan's cultural property laws were extended in 1955 with the establishment of a system by which individuals were designated holders of each of the identified Important Intangible Cultural Properties. These individuals are popularly known as 'Living National Treasures'. Serizawa was appointed a Living National Treasure in 1956 for his *kataezome* (stencil-picture-dyeing), shown in fig. 80. Although *kataezome* is technically the same as other forms of stencil-dyeing, or *katazome*, the term is used to describe the more pictorially expressive work for which Serizawa is famed.

Shimura Fukumi (b.1924) was appointed a Living National Treasure in 1990. Shimura weaves with *tsumugi* silk, although she often uses reeled silk for the warp thread. This combination creates a glossier fabric than that obtained by using *tsumugi* for both weft and warp. Apart from indigo, which is obtained through a specialist supplier, Shimura makes dyes from plants grown in her own garden. The *kimono* in fig. 82 is woven with yarns of indigo blue, yellow derived from eulalia, brown derived from onion skins and

81 *Kimono. Tsumugi* silk
woven with selectively resist-
dyed yarns (*kasuri*). Yūki
(Ibaraki Prefecture), *c*.1960.
147.0 × 127.0.
T.2–1965.

green which is produced by dyeing with eulalia over indigo. Through the use of *tsumugi* silk and the apparent simplicity of the checked design, Shimura combines the traditional characteristics of rural textile design with her own highly sophisticated sense of colour and tone. The titles and imagery of Shimura's textiles reveal her long standing interest in classical Japanese literature. The title of this *kimono*, 'Ise', derives from the tenth-century 'Tales of Ise', one of the most famous works of Japanese literature. These romantic stories of the court noble Ariwara no Narihira (825–880), from the Heian period, featured in much of the work of the Edo-period artists of the Rinpa school. The colours of this *kimono* were inspired by those of Rinpa painting.

Traditional textile techniques are also preserved by various artists whose work is not directly represented under the system of Important Intangible Cultural Properties. Fig. 83 is a *tsumugi* silk *kimono* woven on the island of Amami Ōshima, which is situated between Okinawa and Kyūshū. The traditional colours of Ōshima textiles are the result of repeated immersion in dark mud and the brown iron-rich extract of the *sharinbai* tree. The *kasuri* technique used to pattern Ōshima textiles is taken to a new level of complexity in the work of Tokiemon Fuji (b.1910), seen in fig. 84. The technique he pioneered in the 1970s involves the preliminary weaving of combined strands of thread which are then dyed in narrow strips. The cloth is unravelled and the dyed thread used as either the warp or weft of a finished bolt of fabric. The yarn is dyed so precisely that it is possible to produce crisply defined patterns of great intricacy. In this *kimono* the intensity of both colour and pattern, of auspicious characters, increases down the length of the garment. Designs of this sophistication are worked out carefully in advance using graph paper.

It is interesting that many contemporary Japanese textile artists working in traditional styles use the *kimono* as the primary format for their artistic expression. This is despite the fact that most modern Japanese wear western style dress. Today, with the exception of particular events and professions, only women wear *kimono* and even then at a limited number of formal occasions. While the occurrence of its use has severely diminished, however, the symbolic significance of the *kimono* has intensified. As Japan has come to define itself within the western world over the last one hundred years, the *kimono* has come to mark the boundary with the foreign, to stand for the essence that is Japanese.

82 *Kimono* entitled *Ise*. By Shimura Fukumi (b.1924). *Tsumugi* silk. Kyoto, 1988. 167.5 x 138.0.
FE.11–1989.

83 *Kimono*. *Tsumugi* silk woven with selectively resist-dyed yarns (*kasuri*). Amami Ōshima (Kagoshima Prefecture), *c*.1980. 141.0 × 123.2.
FE.31–1983.

84 *Kimono* entitled *Felicitious Ideography*. By Tokiemom Fuji (b.1910). *Tsumugi* silk, woven with selectively resist-dyed yarns (*kasuri*). Amami Ōshima (Kagoshima Prefecture), 1988. 170.0 × 38.0.
FE.1–1995.

Other forms of traditional textiles are still made to serve more utilitarian purposes, however. Despite the cosmopolitan nature of modern Japan's busy cities, with their high-rise office blocks and large department stores, small shops and restaurants still use *noren*. The example in fig. 85 comes from Kanagawa Prefecture and dates from the 1970s. It is made of indigo-dyed hemp and has a design of fish created with stencils. Fig. 86 is a ramie *noren*, made by Ken'ichi Utsuki (b.1948), who produces a variety of indigo-dyed textiles and garments in his workshop in Kyoto. The design was created by stencilling rice paste over the areas to remain uncoloured, and dip-dyeing the fabric in indigo to produce a light blue shade. The areas to be left this lighter tone were then resisted using the *tsutsugaki* technique, and the fabric was then dipped in the dye bath over fifteen times to produce the rich, dark blue of the background. The calligraphy incorporated into the design reads: '*momo kuri sannen, kaki hachinen*'('one must have patience in all things'). It can also be more literally translated as 'it takes three years for peaches and chestnuts and eight for a persimmon'. These fruits feature in the design.

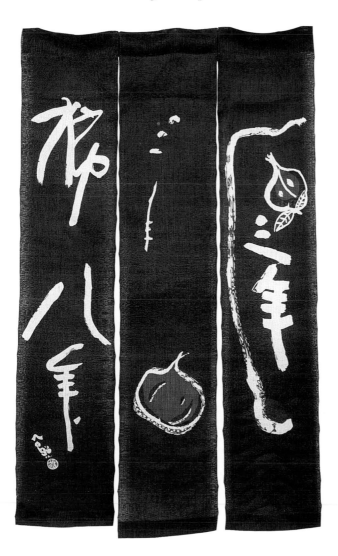

85 Doorway curtain (*noren*). Cotton with stencilled decoration (*katazome*). Kanagawa Prefecture, *c.*1977. 120.6 × 84.0. FE.55–1981.

86 Doorway curtain (*noren*). By Ken'ichi Utsuki (b.1948). Bast fibre (*asa*) with stencilled (*katazome*) and freehand paste-resist decoration (*tsutsugaki*). Kyoto, 1989. 157.5 × 91.8. FE.269–1995.

One form of *kimono* that is still commonly worn in Japan is the *yukata*. These blue and white cotton garments were originally worn after the bath or as nightwear, and are still worn around the home, in hotels and at hot spring resorts. The length of *yukata* fabric in fig. 87, with a stencil-dyed pattern of white against a blue ground, is by Matsubara Yoshichi (b.1937). The complex stencil technique entails not only the careful registering of the paste-resist pattern on both sides of the fabric, but the use of two stencils of different designs. This double stencil technique has enabled Matsubara to create the very detailed pattern of chrysanthemums and dots. The latter result from tiny gaps which remain free of paste when the two stencils are registered. The pattern was created using a pair of Edo-period stencils which were re-cut for Matsubara by a Tokyo-based stencil cutter.

Matsubara learnt his craft in the studio of his father Matsubara Sadakichi (1893–1955), who was appointed a Living National Treasure just before his death. Although brought up in an environment where using traditional techniques was the norm, when he started making his own work Matsubara Yoshichi was not particularly conscious of what such traditions meant. It was only later that he became aware of the historical roots of his techniques and the importance of them.[7] Matsubara has a particular childhood recollection very appropriate to this book. He remembers an occasion when his father's studio was visited by an anthropologist collecting traditional country textiles for various European museums. He asked Matsubara Sadakichi to make him a length of fabric showing the different stages of stencil dyeing. The man's name was Jaap Langewis.[8]

The self-consciously traditional feel of the *yukata* length complements another work by Matsubara in the V&A's collection (fig. 88). The bold contemporary design of this *kimono* has also been created using the stencil-resist indigo dyeing, or *katazome*, technique. Matsubara has developed a very individual

87 Length of fabric. By Matsubara Yoshichi (b.1937). Cotton with stencilled decoration (*katazome*). Tokyo, *c*.1993. 1200.0 × 35.0. FE.286–1995.

88 *Kimono* entitled *Flight*.
By Matsubara Yoshichi (b.1937).
Silk with stencilled decoration
(*katazome*). Tokyo, 1990.
169.0 × 131.0.
FE.10–1995.

method of working which involves the washing off and reapplication of the resist-paste between each of the numerous dippings in the indigo bath. Either the same stencil is moved very slightly, or a set of stencils of the same shape but diminishing size are used. This *kimono* was decorated by the latter method and involved the use of a set of twenty nine stencils (shown in fig. 89). The resulting pattern, in which progressively darker shades of blue emerge from a central area of white, is dazzling in its intensity.

Matsubara's *kimono* was designed primarily as an exhibition piece.[9] Only the very wealthy would be able to buy a garment so painstakingly created by one of the acknowledged masters of contemporary textile design. While Matsubara and others working in this field have a strong awareness of their cultural heritage, they are not necessarily rigid in their adherence to historical precedents. This beautiful garment might have been patterned using traditional methods of indigo stencil-dyeing, but it does not in any way echo nostalgia for an irretrievable past. Now part of the collection at the V&A, this *kimono* is preserved for future generations. While the meaning this garment holds for its audience will change, like all the textiles illustrated in this book it is ultimately invested with the resonance of its own time.

89 Detail of *Flight* with stencils. Stencils of mulberry (*kōzo*) paper. Largest stencil 18.5 × 16.5.
FE.10–1995.

NOTES

1. For an analysis of the role played by western and Japanese style dress in the Meiji and subsequent periods see Liza Dalby, *Kimono: Fashioning Culture* (New Haven and London: Yale University Press 1993).
2. See Satoru Nakamura, 'The Development of Rural Industry' in Chie Nakane and Shinzaburō Ōishi (eds.), op.cit., pp 95–6.
3. For an exploration of the working conditions in the textile industry, see Jean-Piere Lehmann, *The Roots of Modern Japan* (London: Macmillan 1982), pp 206–8 and Barbara Molony, 'Activism Among Women in the Taishō Cotton Textile Industry', in Gail Lee Bernstein (ed.), op.cit., pp 217–38.
4. See Louise Cort, 'The Changing Fortunes of Three Archaic Japanese Textiles', in Annette Weiner and Jane Schneider (eds.), *Cloth and Human Experience* (Washington and London: Smithsonian Institution Press 1991), pp 377–415.
5. Ibid., pp 404–5.
6. Quoted from Rupert Faulkner, *Japanese Studio Crafts: Tradition and the Avant-garde* (London: Laurence King 1995), p.13.
7. This discussion of Matsubara's attitude towards his craft is based on a conversation with the author which took place on 8 June 1995.
8. Although the V&A received so many items from Langewis, sadly this was not one of them.
9. Which is of course its purpose in the V&A. The *kimono* was bought specifically for display in the exhibition *Japanese Studio Textiles: Tradition and the Avant-Garde*, held at the Museum in the summer of 1995.

Selected Bibliography

All the publications listed are in English or have sections translated into English.

Gunhild Avitabile, Eleanor von Erdberg and Robert Moes, *Japanese Folk Art: A Triumph of Simplicity* (New York: Japan Society 1993).

Rev. John Batchelor, *The Ainu and their Folklore* (London: Religious Tract Society 1901).

Gail Lee Bernstein (ed.), *Recreating Japanese Women 1600–1945* (Berkeley, Los Angeles and New York: University of California Press 1991).

Reiko Mochinaga Brandon, *Country Textiles of Japan: The Art of Tsutsugaki* (New York: Weatherhill 1986).

Reiko Mochinaga Brandon and Barbara B. Stephan, *Textile Art of Okinawa* (Honolulu: Honolulu Academy of Arts 1990).

Ciba Review, vol. 4, 1967 (edition devoted to Japanese resist-dyeing techniques).

Louise Cort, 'Three Archaic Japanese Fibres' in Annette Weiner and Jane Schneider (eds.), *Cloth and Human Experience* (Washington and London: Smithsonian Institution Press 1991; original edition 1989), pp 377–415.

Lisa Dalby, *Kimono: Fashioning Culture* (New Haven: Yale University Press 1993).

Edmund de Waal, 'Sōetsu Yanagi', *Crafts*, no. 141, July/August 1996, p.20–21.

Mary Dusenbury, 'Kasuri', *Textile Museum Journal*, vol. 17, 1978, pp 41–64.

Rupert Faulkner, *Japanese Stencils* (London: Victoria and Albert Museum 1988).

Rupert Faulkner, *Japanese Studio Crafts: Tradition and the Avant-Garde* (London: Laurence King 1995).

Mattiebelle Gittlinger, *Masterdyers of the World: Technique and Trade in Early Modern Indian Dyed Cotton Textiles* (Washington: Textile Museum 1982).

Dale Carolyn Gluckman & Sharon Sadako Takeda, *When Art Became Fashion: Kosode in Edo-Period Japan* (Los Angeles and New York: Weatherhill and Los Angeles County Museum of Art 1992).

Victor and Takako Hauge, *Folk Traditions in Japanese Art* (Tokyo: Kōdansha International 1978).

William Hauser, 'The Diffusion of Cotton Processing and Trade in the Kinai Region of Tokugawa Japan', *Journal of Asian Studies*, vol. XXXIII, no.4, August 1974, pp 633–49.

Yoshiko Harada et.al., *Living National Treasures of Japan* (Boston: Boston Museum of Fine Arts 1983).

Money Hickman and Peter Fetchko, *Japan Day by Day: an Exhibition Honoring Edward Sylvester Morse and Commemorating the Hundreth Anniversary of his Arrival in Japan* (Salem: Peabody Museum 1979).

Gensho Sasakura, *Tsutsugaki Textiles of Japan: Traditional Freehand Paste Resist Indigo Dyeing Technique of Auspicious Motifs* (Tokyo: Shikōsha 1987).

Janet Hunter, 'The Meiji Background', in Oliver Impey and Malcolm Fairley (eds.), *Meiji No Takara: Treasures of Imperial Japan* (The Nassar David Khalili Collection of Japanese Art; 5 volumes), vol. 1 *Selected Essays* (London: Kibo Foundation 1995), pp 42–55.

Yūko Kikuchi, 'The Myth of Yanagi's Originality: The Formation of Mingei theory in its Social and Historical Context', *Journal of Design History*, vol. 7, no.4, 1994, pp 247–65.

Japan Textile Colour Design Centre, *Textile Designs of Japan* (Tokyo: Serindia Publications and Kōdansha International 1960).

Josef Kreiner, *Sekai ni Hokoru Ryūkyū ōchō Bunka Ihōten: Yoroppa Amerika Hitsuzō (Treasures of Ryukyuan Art in European Collections)*, (Tokyo: Deutches Institut für Japanstudien 1992).

J. Langewis, 'Geometric Patterns on Japanese Ikats', *Kultuurpatronen*, vol. 2, 1960, pp 79–83.

J. Langewis, 'Japanese Ikat Textiles', *Kultuurpatronen*, vol. 5–6, 1983, pp 74–83.

Jean-Pierre Lehmann, *The Roots of Modern Japan* (London: MacMillan 1982).

Jill Liddell, *The Story of the Kimono* (New York: E.P. Dutton 1989).

Linda Lyton, 'Cotton and the Japanese Popular Textile Tradition', *Arts of Asia*, vol. 24, no. 1, 1994, pp. 60–71.

Lynne Milgram, *Narratives in Cloth: Embroidered Textiles from Aomori, Japan* (Toronto: The Museum for Textiles 1993).

Brian Morean, *Lost Innocence: Folk Craft Potters of Onta, Japan* (Berkeley: University of California Press 1984).

Hugo Munsterberg, *Mingei: Folk Arts of Old Japan* (New York: Asia House Gallery 1965).

Robert Moes and Amanda Mayer Stinchecum, *Mingei: Japanese Folk Art from the Montgomery Collection* (Alexandria, Virginia: Art Services International 1995).

Nihon Mingeikan, *Mingei: Masterpieces of Japanese Folkcraft* (Tokyo and New York: Kōdansha International 1991).

Chie Nakane and Shinzaburō Ōishi, *Tokugawa Japan: The Social and Economic Antecedents of Modern Japan* (Tokyo: University of Tokyo Press 1990).

Sosei Ōshiro and Kanemasa Ashime, *Okinawa Bijutsu Zenshū (The Art of Okinawa)*, vol. 3, *Senshoku (Textiles)*, (Okinawa: Okinawa Times 1989).

William Jay Rathbun, *Beyond the Tanabata Bridge: Traditional Japanese Textiles* (New York: Thames & Hudson in association with the Seattle Art Museum 1993).

Gosta Sandberg, *Indigo Textiles: Technique and History* (London: A&C Black 1989).

Donald Shiveley, 'Sumptuary Regulation and Status in Early Tokugawa Japan', *Harvard Journal of Asiatic Studies*, vol. 25, 1964–5, pp 123–64.

Joan Stanley-Baker, *Mingei: Folk Craft of Japan* (Victoria: Art Gallery of Greater Victoria 1979).

Barbara Stephen, *Japanese Country Textiles* (Toronto: Royal Ontario Museum 1965).

Amanda Mayer Stinchecum, *Kosode: 16th–19th Century Textiles from the Nomura Collection* (New York: Japan Society and Kōdansha International 1984).

Amanda Mayer Stinchecum, 'A Common Thread: Japanese Ikat Textiles', *Asian Art*, vol. III, no. 1, 1990, pp 37–60.

Amanda Mayer Stinchecum, 'Textile Production Under the Poll Tax System in Ryūkyū', *The Textile Museum Journal*, vol. 27–8, 1988–89, pp 57–65.

Jun and Noriko Tomita, *Japanese Ikat Weaving* (London: Routledge and Kegan Paul 1982).

Verity Wilson, 'Country Textiles from Japan and the Ryūkyū Islands in the Victoria and Albert Museum', *Orientations*, vol. 14, no. 7, 1983, pp 28–42.

Yanagi Sōetsu, adapted by Bernard Leach, *The Unknown Craftsman: A Japanese Insight into Beauty* (Tokyo, New York and San Francisco: Kōdansha International, 1989; original edition 1972).

Index